Routledge Revivals

Dinosaur & Co

First published in 1984, *Dinosaur & Co* captures a critical moment in British economic history, when the nation was widely regarded as caught in a chronic process of decline, known as 'de-industrialisation'. At that time, many feared that unless this decline was arrested, Britain would eventually reach a position where it could not export enough to pay for the imports needed to maintain a reasonable standard of living. Tom Lloyd, a leading writer on financial matters, refused to take such a bleakly pessimistic view of the British economy. In this thought-provoking analysis of the British business landscape, Lloyd applies the principles of evolution to the world of business and to its population of companies.

Writing from the vantage point of the mid-1980s, Lloyd makes a testable prediction that over the following two decades the genus company would be forced by changes in its environment to undergo dramatic adaptation. He anticipates that the most conspicuous result of this adaptive activity would be the emergence of the small, high technology company as the dominant corporate species and the gradual disappearance of the giant companies that dominated the era. Lloyd recounts seven stories of UK companies and the entrepreneurs who ran them, providing anecdotal evidence about how well Britain was equipped to ride out this evolutionary upheaval. In a final section, he draws together the common threads running through the book, considering the implications of his arguments and the evidence, and concluding by discussing the problem of the prevailing anti-business attitude in Britain.

Dinosaur & Co offers readers a fascinating historical lens through which to examine the transformation of British business and the lasting questions about industrial evolution and economic adaptation.

Dinosaur & Co

Studies in Corporate Evolution

Tom Llyod

Routledge
Taylor & Francis Group

First published in 1984
by Routledge & Kegan Paul plc

This edition first published in 2026 by Routledge
4 Park Square, Milton Park, Abingdon, Oxon, OX14 4RN

and by Routledge
605 Third Avenue, New York, NY 10158

Routledge is an imprint of the Taylor & Francis Group, an informa business

A Library of Congress record exists under LCCN: 83016094

ISBN: 978-1-041-35408-6 (hbk)
ISBN: 978-1-003-79763-0 (ebk)
ISBN: 978-1-041-35428-4 (pbk)

Book DOI 10.4324/9781003797630

Tom Lloyd

DINOSAUR & CO

Studies in corporate evolution

Routledge & Kegan Paul
London, Boston, Melbourne and Henley

First published in 1984
by Routledge & Kegan Paul plc

39 Store Street, London WC1E 7DD, England

9 Park Street, Boston, Mass. 02108, USA

464 St Kilda Road,
Melbourne, Victoria 3004, Australia and

Broadway House, Newtown Road,
Henley-on-Thames, Oxon RG9 1EN, England

Phototypeset by Input Typesetting Ltd, London
Printed in Great Britain by
Billing & Sons, Worcester

Library of Congress Cataloging in Publication Data

Lloyd, Tom.
Dinosaur & Co: studies in corporate evolution.

Includes index.
1. Corporations—Great Britain. 2. High technology industries—Great Britain. 3. Great Britain—Industries. I. Title. II. Title: Dinosaur and Company. III. Title: Dinosaur & Company.
HD2845.L64 1984 338.7'4'0941 83–16094
British Library CIP available

ISBN 0–7100–9933–9

Contents

Plates

Between pp. 118–19

To Eva, Kate and Owen for their patience

Acknowledgments

This book was planned and written over a period of two years, during which time I was an employee at *Financial Weekly*. I would like to thank two editors, Stephen Hugh-Jones and Ray Heath, for their indulgence and encouragement, the staff of *Financial Weekly* for their advice and help and my friends, particularly David Fraser, Jon May, David Smith and Wout Woltz, for stimulating discussion and helpful criticism.

Most of all I would like to thank the protagonists in my stories. They are busy people. It was kind of them to spare me some of their valuable time.

Introduction

This book is an attempt to apply the principles of evolution to the world of business and to its population of companies.

It is divided into three parts, the first of which makes the testable prediction that over the next two decades or so the genus 'company' will be forced by changes in its environment to undergo dramatic adaptation. The most conspicuous result of this adaptive activity will be the emergence of the small, high-technology company as the dominant corporate species and the gradual disappearance of today's giant companies.

Part II is an attempt to provide some anecdotal evidence about how well Britain is equipped to ride out this evolutionary upheaval. It consists of seven stories of UK companies and the entrepreneurs who run them. I must emphasise that all expressions of opinion and judgment in these chapters are, except where expressly attributed to others, my own. Though I found in the entrepreneurs I spoke to broad agreement with many of my ideas (indeed, my views are to some extent a reflection of theirs), it should not be assumed that my analysis of what these entrepreneurs have done is the same in all cases as theirs.

The final part of the book is an attempt to draw together some of the common threads that have run through the earlier chapters. Here again, all value judgments are my own. I make a number of policy prescriptions in chapter 10 and in the final chapter I attempt the difficult task of promoting the entrepreneur a few rungs up the ladder of social status. I must own to a prejudice acquired while working on this book: I like entrepreneurs. I have met a fair number of them. I find all of them interesting, stimulating and amusing.

I would very much like this book to be read by young people. If it persuades just one of them to stomach prejudices about entrepreneurs less positive than mine, and to set up his or her own company, then my time, and that of all those who have helped me with this book, will not have been entirely wasted.

PART I

Corporate catastrophe

1
The corporate dinosaurs

The triumph of scale

One of the greatest errors of our age is the belief that the giant company represents the crowning and culminating glory of capitalist evolution. It is a belief held not only by the leaders of the giant companies themselves on each of whom depends the livelihoods of tens of thousands of people and the deployment of hundreds of millions of pounds of finance – it is held by many smaller companies who wish to be larger, by governments who find it convenient to deal with the few and the powerful, by the unions whose own evolution has reflected that of their natural opponents and by the people at large who have learned to associate big companies and their standardised products with greater efficiency and therefore lower prices.

They may disagree on many things, on who should own the corporate mammoths, on how democratically they should be run, on what means should be used to control them or on how heavily they should be taxed, but all agree that when it comes to economic efficiency in industry and to sheer productive capacity, the giant corporations are the highest form of life.

There have been voices raised in dissent. The post-industrialists of the late 1960s and the consumer movement of the 1970s both challenged, in their different ways, the goal of economic growth and development. The late E. F. Schumacher made an impassioned plea in his book *Small is Beautiful* for a new approach to economics 'as if people mattered'.

The dissenters, though, never dispute the claim of the large corporations to efficiency; rather they reject the deification of efficiency on the grounds that it is robbing the world of fraternity, cleanliness, quiet and contentment.

Throughout the long debate on the desirability of economic growth, the principle of 'economies of scale', which states that companies become more efficient as they grow larger, has gone unchallenged. It has acquired the status of an axiom in the system of economic thought. The 'diseconomies' of scale the dissenters find so distasteful are not economic diseconomies at all, but social ones.

And so the giant corporations, castigated for their brutally single-minded search for profit, condemned for their amorality and despised heartily for their greed, remain at least the objects of economic approbation. They continue to be regarded as the most highly evolved form of business life.

The reptilian catastrophe

The dinosaurs were highly evolved. The basic blueprint from which they emerged first appeared in the early Permian period about 275 million years ago. During the subsequent 200 million years the design was refined and progressively scaled-up by the process of natural selection, arriving eventually at the largest land animals the world has ever seen.

And then, 65 million years ago, just before the dawn of the Tertiary period, a mysterious catastrophe struck. During a span of centuries, no more than a moment in the geological time-scale, the dinosaurs disappeared.

One way of looking at this extraordinary extinction is to regard the dinosaurs as the victims of their own excessive evolution. They exploited natural selection so extravagantly that when the time came there was insufficient potential for variation in their gene pool for them to adapt to an abruptly changed environment.

Until that time the trend towards giantism was an appropriate adaptive response – there were, if you like, biological economies of scale. After the great dying at the end of the Cretaceous period, warm blood and much smaller size proved a more successful combination of qualities.

Whether the catastrophe which eclipsed the dinosaurs took the form of a flood or an ice age, or whether it was caused by the impact on the Earth of a large object which changed the climate or whether it was because of a sudden restlessness in the Earth's crust (continental drift), is still unclear.

What matters is that something happened and that it can be called catastrophic only in retrospect, because of what happened to the dinosaurs. It was a catastrophe for the dinosaurs – it was more like a blessing in disguise for the mammals.

And it is important to recognise that in evolutionary biology, in mathematics and increasingly these days in economics, the word 'catastrophe' has acquired a somewhat technical meaning. In Catastrophe Theory the word describes not the event of common usage which could take any form, but the sequence of events leading up to and proceeding from a critical point. Catastrophe Theory is an attempt to analyse the way in which a previously stable system can reach a point of chronic instability, a 'cusp' point, which leads to a total collapse of the old order (dinosaur domination) and subsequently to the emergence of a new stability of a very different kind (mammal domination).

Science and business – allies or rivals

No doubt all this talk of dinosaurs and catastrophes in the context of modern business sounds a mite fanciful, even melodramatic.

Most people would accept that we are experiencing a period of very rapid technological advance, particularly in the fields of microelectronics and biotechnology. Most people would probably accept that the impact of these changes on everyday life is likely to be profound, even revolutionary.

Indeed, there is general agreement that the advent of the microchip heralds the 'second industrial revolution' and that over the next decade or so, biotechnology will become as important, if not more so. But to acknowledge the imminence of a transformation in the way we live and work does not, at first sight anyway, imply a belief that the corporate system must change in any fundamental way.

In the Western world companies are regarded as the vehicles

for the spread of technological advance. They are the means by which knowledge of commercial significance is disseminated and exploited. Companies act as the medium of change; there seems to be no reason to expect them to partake of the substance of change. The twentieth century has, after all, witnessed one technological revolution already, in the application of the discoveries of nuclear physics, and this has had little effect on corporate structures. If anything, the age of nuclear weapons and nuclear energy has actually strengthened the tendency towards great size in the corporate world.

Size brings with it market strength both as buyer and seller; it facilitates the accumulation of massive financial resources which in their turn permit an extensive spreading of risk between a number of diverse activities; it also provides political influence – the ability to change the commercial environment in beneficial ways which is so vital for large companies these days as governments take upon themselves the task of economic management.

The utility of these modern economies of scale does not appear to be reduced in any way by technological developments. It has always been assumed that the business world exists in parallel with the world of science and technology. The two areas of activity are supposed to be naturally symbiotic, enjoying a mutually advantageous relationship while maintaining their own distinctive functional natures.

Scientists discover and businessmen exploit – it has always been so. Why should it change now?

The scientist/entrepreneur

The functional distinction between science and business remains intact but the corresponding distinction on the personal level, which once separated very clearly the world of the businessman from the world of the scientist, has begun to fade.

A growing number of scientists and engineers are emigrating to the business world and it is becoming apparent that their preferred habitat there is the small company.

With very few exceptions, large companies have been conspicuously absent in recent years from the frontiers of technological advance. The important breakthroughs in microelectronics and biotechnology over the past two decades or so have come not from the universities or the research establishments of the giant corporations, but from small groups of talented scientists and engineers working for companies in which they are substantial shareholders – working, in effect, for themselves. When technology is advancing rapidly the technologists and scientists become very important people. They command a high price in the marketplace.

With increasing frequency these first-division brains are withdrawing themselves from the job market altogether and instead are setting up in competition with those very same companies which might previously have become their employers. An essential quality of the scientific mind is its openness. Without that openness those rare flashes of insight, the sudden connections between hitherto unrelated concepts which are the stuff of scientific inspiration, simply do not occur.

A scientist who decides to become a businessman does so because he has made a connection between what he is doing in his laboratory and what the world out there wants or will want. The connection is his first entrepreneurial thought and it is no different in kind from the sort of connections which go to make up scientific inspirations.

In a sense, therefore, the scientists who come to the business game come pre-trained. The training is unorthodox by business school standards but the essential elements are there: the alertness to opportunity, the unwillingness to take the conventional wisdom for granted, the patience and perseverance to do the hard, boring graft needed to turn an insight into a publishable discovery or into a marketable product.

It should not be too surprising to find that some scientists turn out to be very good businessmen.

And by the standards of microelectronics and biotechnology, the science of business, to the extent that business is a science, is not intellectually demanding. The concepts are relatively straightforward, the arithmetic is simple and for men and women who were introduced to computers at school, the technology of modern business must be reassuringly familiar.

The blurring of roles at the frontier dividing the science and business worlds is producing a new kind of scientist and a new kind of businessman. Science is often being done these days for a different reason or at least with a different conception of its ultimate goal. In a way these pin-striped PhDs are not abandoning science at all when they go into business but are merely widening its scope. Their search for knowledge has become a search for marketable knowledge.

For these reasons it makes sense to think of the entrepreneurial scientists as comprising a new species of commercial animal. They are not scientists primarily and neither are they businessmen – they embrace both of the traditionally separated functions. I shall call them the scientist/entrepreneurs.

An important feature of the scientist/entrepreneur is that he has evolved from the parent tradition of only one of the two functions he embodies. Businessmen do not, as a rule, become scientists; the traffic is strictly one way. That is why it makes sense to talk in terms of a catastrophic change. A process has begun which is upsetting the traditional balance between science and business. The system is becoming unstable.

Things get no better for the business establishment when one considers the position of scientists already working for the giant corporations in the research and development centres. It might be argued that these people will act as a counter-balance to the emergent scientist/entrepreneurs. Perhaps some loyal company scientists will fulfil that role. Others, though, are bound to be infected by the same desires for wealth, independence and excitement which are seducing talent away from the universities. Each time a scientist/entrepreneur launches his company on the share market and becomes a multi-millionaire in the process, the loyalty of corporation scientists is tested a little more.

Some of the more enlightened giant corporations have become aware of this danger and are attempting to erect barriers against this egress. They are trying to bind their key people to them by paying them more and offering some of the inducements available in small companies.

High salaries, generous perks, the promise of a fat pension, the 'emoluments package' offered to senior research personnel – these can help a large company to keep its best people for a while. In the end though many of the best will become aware of their true worth to their employers. They will begin to demand a 'piece of the action' (a share of the profits they generate) and if they do not get it they will leave, often taking valuable and non-patentable knowledge about technologies and product-development strategies with them.

Large companies can offer stock options or share incentive schemes to key personnel (to the extent that their institutional shareholders permit) but precisely because they are large, the equity they can offer is too dilute to represent much of an incentive to the ambitious scientist.

The effect an individual discovery can have on a large company's profits is seldom much more than marginal. Share analysts in the oil sector use the word 'exposure' to indicate the degree to which a company's worth, and hence its share price, is likely to be affected by an oil discovery.

Almost invariably, investment in a small company, with a tiny stake in an exploration consortium, offers a much greater potential for capital gain than does investment in a larger company whose exploration risks are better spread but whose 'exposure' to success in any one exploration venture is strictly limited. A scientific discovery or an engineering breakthrough is similar in this respect to an oil discovery. It normally makes very little difference to a large company, but it can transform a small one.

And other things being equal, a scientist or engineer will obviously prefer to own a piece of the action in a company whose success he can play a significant part in, than stock in a large group whose share price reflects the influence of a thousand other factors quite remote from his laboratory. Only in this way will the entrepreneurially-minded scientist maximise the financial exposure of his skills in the marketplace.

There is one other siren song that is luring good scientists and engineers away from the large companies and towards small ones – it is the generally greater scientific freedom enjoyed in small companies. It is in the interests of small companies to offer their key scientific staff a wide intellectual space to work in. Their success depends on their ability to establish a technological lead and it does not matter much precisely what form that lead takes.

Large companies have in mind much more specific research objectives when they hire scientists, objectives which reflect the organisation's history, its traditional markets, its non-research skills, its financial resources and, most important of all, the strategic thinking of its top management. Scientists are employed by large companies to do a job; they are not employed to be creative in a general sense.

A biologist hired by a large brewing group, for example, will be expected to devote his time to improving the position of that group in the beer market either by developing a better beer or by discovering a more efficient brewing process.

If that same scientist becomes deeply fascinated by the micro-organisms which power the process of fermentation, and if he develops important ideas of his own about ways in which yeasts and fermentation methods could be used to make a multitude of other products each as different from beer as chalk is from cheese, he will soon become frustrated.

His curiosity, which is one of the qualities that distinguishes him from other men and women, will come up against the product and marketing prejudices of his employer and will meet stern resistance. Large companies can seldom afford to indulge the curiosity of their scientists.

A scientist in such a position, and at a time like the present of explosive scientific advance there are likely to be many such, is faced with two options: he can return to pursue his new interests at university or he can seek employment or partnership with a young company unburdened by firm commitments to particular products and markets.

In this way the ranks of the new genus 'scientist/entrepreneur' are being filled by flows from two different sources: from the universities which cannot offer the financial rewards or the excitement of a business life and from big business which is incapable of providing the kind of inducements or status the scientists now feel they deserve or the freedom to explore all the lines of research which catch their fancy.

Together these two classes of refugee scientist represent a considerable threat to the business establishment; a threat to which there is no obviously effective response.

Industrial disintegration

Over the past few years the neologism 'unbundling' has come into vogue in business circles.

The word describes the process of extracting a particular business activity from a 'bundle' of activities previously carried out by a single organisation and then establishing that activity as a separate specialisation in its own right. Most of those who use the word imagine the phenomenon applies only to the service sector and assume it to be a relatively minor symptom of the service industry's growth.

But as a number of writers have pointed out (e.g. Jonathan Gershuny in *The Self-Service Economy*), most of the growth in service activity since the war has taken place in manufacturing industry. So although 'unbundling' can be said to be associated primarily with service *activity*, it is far from being confined solely to the service *industry*.

The computer software industry was exhibiting classic 'unbundling' characteristics long before the word was even coined. It is of particular interest because it does not fit comfortably into either of the two main industrial classifications, service or manufacturing.

For the purposes of national statistics gathering, software activity is normally grouped under the main heading of 'computer services' and is hence regarded as part of the service industry, alongside time-sharing, systems analysis, consultancy, etc. Those responsible for the preparation of the national accounts have to put software somewhere and it undeniably bears a superficial resemblance to other computer services if only because, like them, it has nothing directly to do with the manufacture of computers themselves.

But these days the software industry exhibits many of the features of traditional manufacturing industry. The large software houses sell complete computer systems of which the hardware is merely a component like a Japanese-made engine might be a component of a British Leyland car. At this level software is much more than mere hardware packaging.

And at the lower end of the scale there is, in the 'off-the-shelf' software package, something very akin to the mass-produced consumer durable good. It is like a book in that it only has to be written once and at the same time like a camera or radio in that it can be used over and over again.

The mass-market features of the software 'good' are becoming increasingly evident as the microcomputer establishes itself as a consumer durable of a rather more familiar kind. To classify the software industry as a service industry is like classifying the long-playing record industry and the pre-recorded cassette tape industry as service industries, which clearly they are not.

This mis-classification of software is more than just a statistical oddity. Governments concoct industrial strategies on the basis of the gross features of the economy revealed in the national accounts. If the most dynamic industry of our time continues to be regarded as akin to banking or tourism, serious policy errors may result.

As we shall see in later chapters, independent software houses have been a feature of the British computer industry from quite early on; one could say that to some extent the software product was born 'unbundled' from the hardware industry in Britain.

This was certainly not the case in Japan, however, and yet in the spring and early summer of 1981 (see *The Economist*, 11.7.81), a veritable unbundling spasm contorted the traditionally conservative Japanese software industry. In the space of a few months no less than 40 programmers working for the big shipbuilding and machine tool group Ishikawajima-Harima Heavy Industries left to form their own company when top management decided to shut down the group's software sales operation. The top brass wanted the programmers to concentrate purely on the group's own data-processing requirements.

A year earlier a similar mass defection denuded the medium-sized Hokushin Electric of its software staff. Japan at last seems to be developing the sort of privateering software industry common to other industrialised countries, the lack of which has meant that until now the Japanese software market has been dominated by US imports.

That such developments should be taking place within a business culture which lays great stress on employee loyalty, where lifetime employment with a single firm is the almost universal rule and where, consequently, labour mobility has traditionally been so low as to be virtually negligible, bears witness to the power of the unbundling forces at work.

The phenomenon is evident elsewhere too. In the British retailing industry the so-called 'food brokers' have unbundled some of the traditional wholesale and marketing functions. In manufacturing industry specialist design houses have assumed the role, in some cases, of the 'in-house' product development department. There is also a growing tendency for the manufacture of independently conceived products to be sub-contracted to specialist engineering firms.

A case in point is the Timex factory in Dundee. Having become resigned to the disappearance of the market for its main product the mechanical clock, Timex has set itself up as a bespoke manufacturing operation. It has made the Nimslo camera, the Sinclair microcomputers and the new range of Sinclair flat-screen televisions. All these products were conceived and developed independently of Timex.

Unbundling is best regarded as an example of a more general disintegrative process at work in modern industry which also includes such phenomena as 'de-mergers' and 'management buy-outs'. Together they represent the lumps of rock tumbling down the industrial mountainside, dislodged by the growing power of the technological earthquake.

Unbundling know-how

Nowhere is the process of industrial disintegration more evident than in the high-technology industries. Unbundling is taking place there on a grand scale.

Consider the recent emergence of the so-called 'concept' companies: small groups of the best brains in a particular field who attempt to develop whole technologies, not caring too much where that development leads them so long as there is money to be made there.

The concept company is typically a partnership between gifted scientists and imaginative businessmen. In a sense it can be regarded as the result of lifting a successful research team out of its natural university habitat and dumping it down in the middle of the business world. Once there, it begins to compete with conventional businesses in a very unconventional way.

Normally when a new company enters a particular market, it takes the market as given and devotes its efforts to supplying that market with the usual range of goods or services at a competitive price. It is the ability of the new company to contain its costs sufficiently to be able to charge a competitive price for its products which determines whether or not the company will succeed.

Concept companies could not care less about price. They are interested solely in establishing a technological lead over their rivals. Nor are they particularly interested in supplying an existing market with familiar goods; they are much more concerned with supplying technology capable of making a completely new type of product for a market which may not even exist yet.

Bob Noyce, founder of Intel and co-inventor of the Integrated Circuit, spelled out some of the implications of this new style of competition in an article in the *Scientific American* (vol. 237, no. 3):

> In an industry whose product declines in price by 25% a year the motivation for doing research is clearly high. A year's advantage in introducing a new product or new process can give a company a 25% cost advantage over competing companies: conversely, a year's lag puts a company at a significant disadvantage with respect to its competitors. Product development is a critical part of company strategy and product obsolescence is a fact of life. The return on successful investment in research and development is great and so is the penalty for failure. The leading producers of integrated circuits spend approximately 10% of their sales income on research and development. In a constant price environment one could say that investment for research and development buys an annuity paying $2.50 per year for each dollar invested! Clearly most of this annuity is either paid out to the purchasers of integrated circuits or reflected in price reductions that are necessary to develop new markets.

The biotechnology concept companies are also good examples of the breed. A number of them have become highly successful in a very short space of time without ever having sold a single, conventional product. Instead they have sold knowledge. They have developed a lead in an important new technology and have established proprietary rights in that technology – rights which they are beginning to sell to ordinary businesses in the chemical and pharmaceutical sectors.

There are various ways of selling knowledge. It can be packaged in the form of a licensing agreement (licensing is common in the microchip industry because of the desire of chip users for a 'second source' of the components to ensure security of supply); the transactions can take the form of a research contract taken out by a 'downstream' company with a concept company, or a general right of access to a particular area of a concept company's research can be bought which amounts to a subcontracting of research effort.

By whatever means the scientist/entrepreneurs turn their lead to their advantage, the result is the same – a transfer of wealth from the company buying the knowledge to the company supplying it.

The economics of the information market are complex and as yet poorly understood. However, it is already clear that a substantial element of what economists call monopoly profit or 'rent' tends to accrue to the knowledge-supplying company so long as that company maintains its technological lead.

This is new. Previously the monopoly profit on exclusive knowledge went to the big companies either through the relatively easy access they had to university research or by virtue of their ownership of the rights to discoveries made by their own scientists. Nowadays the situation is rather different. Small, high-technology companies are beginning to disaggregate or 'unbundle' the monopoly profit associated with knowledge itself from the more normal profits associated with the exploitation of knowledge.

One of two things can happen then. The small company can use its monopoly profits to invest in the research needed to establish a lead in the next generation of products or the scientist/entrepreneurs can set up shop in competition with their erstwhile customers. When that happens the knowledge the big companies need to stay ahead of the game will cease to be offered for sale to the highest bidder. Big companies will then be in a fix. And even if the giant corporations are alive to the danger, it is hard to see what they can do about it apart from trying to reach an agreement amongst themselves to boycott the small, knowledge-supplying companies which would seem a hopeless endeavour.

The difficulty for the big companies is that business economics have changed. It was the need to remain price competitive which encouraged companies to grow large in the first place; once that need disappears, or rather once that need becomes subordinate to the need to maintain a technological lead, size itself becomes a relatively redundant quality.

Other qualities become much more important; qualities which encourage vigorous and successful research, which win the loyalty of key scientific and technical personnel, which produce the commercial agility and flexibility needed to keep abreast and in front of developments in science and in the marketplace . . . in short, qualities which add up to adaptability in a business world caught in an extraordinary spasm of scientific advance.

Small companies have these qualities; large companies do not. The parallel with the dinosaurs, caught in all their magnificence on the edge of catastrophe, is inescapable.

The paradox of size and growth

The great corporate dying of the late twentieth and early twenty-first centuries will take many forms. Some large companies will go out of business, others will split apart into smaller units – there has already been a spate of 'de-mergers' and 'management buy-outs' – and there will be a host of re-structurings, re-arrangements and re-alignments.

Whole industries are dying and being born. Some may be unrecognisable in a decade or so after the pressures of technology and of market evolution have forced them to twist and turn, abandoning activities here while building them up there, in their attempts to survive in a rapidly changing environment.

But individual companies are never likely to be so big again as some of them are now, while technological advance maintains its present pace (it is more likely to accelerate). I believe that in retrospect the giant corporations of the late twentieth century will be seen as the culmination of the integrating tendency in business and that hereafter the diseconomies of scale will tend to constrict the flow of growth sap at a much earlier stage in a company's development.

There is a paradox here – perhaps there always was and it has taken the advent of the scientist/entrepreneur to make it apparent. Companies, especially high-technology companies, cannot afford not to grow. Great size and stultifying bureaucracy alienate the commercially significant mind, but so do stagnation and a lack of the adventurous spirit.

Companies will have to reconcile themselves to the fact that they will lose their key people if they do not grow and that if they do grow, they will lose their key people. The trick will be to get the timing right. Companies must aim to hire good people just before they begin to do their best work.

Theory Z

I want to conclude this opening chapter with a brief description of what I believe to be the most powerful argument against the 'Dinosaur & Co' thesis.

It is known as 'Theory Z' and though I do not believe it has been proposed before as a defence available to big business against the challenge of smaller and more agile rivals, it seems to me to offer the most promising adaptive response for large corporations in these 'catastrophic' times.

Theory Z is the invention of Dr William Ouchi, a professor at the University of California's Graduate School of Management. Ouchi's argument is that American companies will only be able to meet successfully the challenge of the giant Japanese corporations in world markets if they adopt elements of the Japanese management style.

He regards the Japanese and American management styles as being the creatures of their respective national cultures. In America the cultural emphasis is on the individual whereas in Japan it is on the collective or the group; the American culture tends to generate specialists while the Japanese culture produces generalists.

In business this translates in the US into a stratified management population. There is much more mobility in America within management functions and hence between companies. When a sales manager in a US company decides it is time for a change he is more likely to move to another company than to become a data-processing manager or a budget controller in the same company.

In Japanese companies the situation is quite the reverse. There is a tradition of life-time employment with the same company and of a high degree of functional mobility within the company. Managers tend to get moved around frequently, acquiring over time quite a good overall view of how things are done in almost every area.

The great advantage of this system, according to Dr Ouchi, is that it leads to the emergence of a common philosophy about what the company is and about what it should be doing. All decisions are taken in the context of this philosophy and no decision is taken until it has been discussed in detail with everyone who will be affected by it.

The result is a high degree of corporate loyalty, strong commitment at all levels to the business plan and to any changes made to it, far less time and effort wasted on bickering and 'politicking' and consequently, much higher productivity. But Dr Ouchi does not pass any snap judgment about which system is better. He points out that there are advantages to the American system too; it makes for greater expertise and inventiveness and ensures the more rapid dissemination of new skills and technologies throughout the economy.

Dr Ouchi says that in addition to the 'Type A' (American) and 'Type J' (Japanese) organisations and their associated management styles there is a third type of organisation, 'Type Z', which incorporates the best features of both the American and Japanese systems.

His book *Theory Z – how American business can meet the Japanese challenge* caused quite a stir when it was published in the US in 1981. It was not long before a number of companies began to describe themselves as 'Theory Z' organisations.

I think Ouchi is quite right to attribute Japan's economic success to her management methods. I also think he is right to propose that Western companies try to adopt a management style along the lines of 'Theory Z' as he describes it. However, I think he is wrong to suggest that this sort of style is alien to the American culture; that it could only have evolved in a collective, generalist culture like Japan's and not in any individualistic, specialist culture of the Western kind.

For it is clear to me that Z-type management styles *have* evolved in the West; that they are, in fact, very common here. Theory Z describes to a 'T' the way in which small businesses are run.

The interesting question is why do Western companies and organisations lose this intimate, consensus style of management, based on mutual trust and common goals, as they grow larger? What are the forces which compel Theory Z styles to degenerate as the company grows, into the stratified, hierarchical pattern common to most large businesses in the West?

I do not know the answer to that question, but I can offer an evolutionary interpretation of the phenomenon.

One could say that the Japanese big business management style is more highly evolved than the West's because it has succeeded in retaining to maturity a desirable quality of the standard small-business management style; a quality that in the West tends to disappear as the company matures.

Evolutionary biologists will recognise this process as an example of an important evolutionary mechanism known as 'neoteny'. I shall return to the idea of neoteny later (see page 37); it raises a number of interesting questions for corporate evolution.

But what of the effect of Dr Ouchi's theory on the Dinosaur & Co thesis? Does it really offer to large companies an adequate defence against the forces of corporate disintegration?

Time will tell, but personally I doubt it. The main corporate challenge now is the sheer speed of technological advance, and in these circumstances the specialist, individualist qualities promoted by the Western culture are just as valuable. The adoption by a large company of a Theory Z style may help it to keep key people from leaving for a little while, but the small companies will be Theory Z too.

I expect tomorrow's successful companies to be smaller because of the reasons I have given and I expect them to be managed in a way that corresponds very closely with Dr Ouchi's Theory Z.

It is perhaps worth noting, *en passant*, that an implication of all this is that Western businesses will not have to worry much longer about the Japanese challenge. The Japanese business style does not seem to me to be very well adapted to cope with the competitive conditions that prevail in the era of rapid technological advance.

2
California dreamers

The road to San José

California is a part of the world where the future seems to emerge with more frequency than elsewhere. Whether this is because of some fundamental quality of the region, perhaps the effect on the communal psyche of California's delicate geology, or because of the sort of people who are attracted to the place, is hard to say.

The aura is unmistakable though – an openness, a willingness to experiment, a refusal to take social, economic or technical conventions for granted; a peculiar kind of frontier mentality which, perhaps because it finds itself located on the edge of a wide ocean, has turned in on itself and become pre-occupied with non-geographical forms of exploration and adventure.

Once a place earns a reputation like that, those special qualities tend to become self-reinforcing. For scientists and engineers, California is a place where discovery and achievement hang tantalisingly in the air, where good work can be done, where the smallest kernel of genius is sure to be teased out of a person and then generously rewarded.

I imagine driving south from San Francisco along Highway 101. The weather is bright and warm – the air slightly humid. I cruise around the margin of Fr'isco Bay and follow the road east as it skirts the navy airfield at Moffett near Palo Alto. I do not know whether I can see Xerox Corporation's Palo Alto laboratories from the road, but I glimpse them in my mind's eye – low, white buildings with much brown tinted glass.

I drive on southwards towards San José, through the fertile lowlands of the Santa Clara Valley. On my left the wooded slopes of the Monte Bello ridge obscure my view of the sea.

I watch an azure blue Learjet side-slip down across the foothills of the Diablo Range as it begins its approach to the small airfield near the roadside. Another plane is just taking off with a roar of full thrust. It heads eastwards, making for New York, carrying the marketing Vice-President or perhaps the chief executive of some local company, who has with him a new electronic device which he will demonstrate to East Coast customers.

My eyes return to ground level. Amidst the few remaining peach orchards and citrus plantations in the Santa Clara Valley I see avenues of neat, timber-framed houses surrounded by well-groomed lawns and brightly-flowering shrubs. Interspersed between the residential areas are low, single-storey factory complexes, or perhaps they should be called laboratory complexes. The traditional features of the factory – the size, the smoke, the noise, the dirt, the incessant comings and goings of delivery trucks and container lorries, are wholly absent. It takes an effort of will to accept that in this place, along either side of that stretch of Highway 101 which links Palo Alto with San José, the tools of the second industrial revolution are being forged.

William Blake spoke of 'dark Satanic mills'. It is said he was referring to the universities of the late nineteenth century and to the de-humanising scientific method they taught after the pattern suggested by Francis Bacon. For most people, though, Blake's phrase evokes images of the noisy, grimy, spiritually impoverished, multi-storey textile mills and iron foundries which more than a century ago were dragging the world by the scruff of its neck into the machine age.

There is nothing remotely resembling those monolithic, brutally intrusive features of the early industrial landscape in Santa Clara Valley, better known to the outside world as 'Silicon Valley'. If an industrial revolution is in progress here it is of a very different kind from the one whose smog-shrouded images still dominate popular conception.

To understand the true nature of this new industrial revolution a more subtle imagination is required. The coarse and brutal vitality of a nineteenth-century textile mill is no paradigm here.

There is vitality in the Santa Clara Valley in abundance, but it is quiet, cerebral and often downright secretive. What manufacturing activity there is here is not noisy and, above all, it is not dirty. On the contrary, great pains are taken to make the manufacturing areas of Silicon Valley electronics companies scrupulously clean. Factory workers tip-toe around the 'clean rooms' dressed in sanitised white coats, wearing disposable paper coveralls on their heads and feet. Dandruff from hair and dust from boots can play merry hell with evaporation and etching processes.

Fritz Lang's vision of industrial conditions in the future, depicted in his film *Metropolis*, are absent outside the clean rooms too.

Laboratory images are much more appropriate. White-gowned figures sit at benches peering down microscopes and manipulating strange, robot-like tools. These are the high-precision soldering machines used to attach hair-thin gold filaments to the tiny slivers of silicon which are super-complex electronic circuits. From time to time the high-pitched whine of a diamond-tipped, wafer thin circular saw can be heard as it separates the microcircuits that have been etched into thin slices of silicon crystal.

The visible scale of this industrial revolution is tiny by comparison with the first, but its power is even more awesome. A hundred years ago the smoke and noise which hammered and heated was the accompaniment of the extension of muscle-power. Today, here in California, in quietness and cleanliness, human brainpower is being distilled and frozen. Knowledge is being made objective.

Downstream from these chip factories, the subsequent processing stages are even more at odds with the usual conception of industrial engineering. As the chips themselves are flown to the other side of the world to be encased in brown ceramic material, the teaching masters will set about the task of bringing these slivers of densely packed logic to life. The writers of 'assembler', 'compiler' and the higher-level computer languages will not change the chips at all, they will merely instruct them – the task of the software smiths is to add function to logic; to pile brainpower on brainstuff.

And it is in the software industry, where thought alone is both raw material and product, that the next chapter of industrial history will be written. It will be the programmers and not the chipmakers who will create the first genuinely thoughtful machines.

In the beginning there was Shockley

California was not the birthplace of the electronic age. It began far away in the mind of a cold and awkward genius called William Bradford Shockley. The man has since achieved a certain notoriety amongst liberal elements in society because of his preoccupation with eugenics and the credence he gives to dubious theories concerning racial differences in intelligence.

Shockley was born of English-American parents in London on 13 February 1910. He graduated from the California Institute of Technology in 1932 and obtained his PhD from the Massachusetts Institute of Technology in 1936. Three years later, while working at Bell Laboratories on America's east coast, he wrote the following entry in his diary, datelined 29 December 1939: 'It has today occurred to me that an amplifier using semiconductors rather than vacuum is in principle possible.'

This intellectual bomb, which was later to explode with quiet but devastating power in the industrialised world, lay unarmed in Shockley's mind throughout the Second World War during most of which Shockley was engaged in operations research at the Pentagon.

After the war Shockley returned to Bell Labs as joint leader of a semiconductor research team. His two most illustrious collaborators were Dr John Bardeen and Dr Walter Brattain. In November 1947, after many false starts and frustrations, the final hurdle was cleared. Brattain and another member of the team, Dr Robert Gibney, devised a way of unblocking a particularly solid electron log-jam which was preventing the semiconductor material they were working with from performing in the way they wished. After that the work went swiftly and within a month a device which TRANSferred current across a resISTOR was born.

Not even Shockley could have conceived of the full significance of his invention of the transistor in 1947. Certainly none of his contemporaries were aware of what had happened. The first transistors were expensive and unreliable, and it was not until 1956 that Shockley, Bardeen and Brattain journeyed to Stockholm to receive a Nobel Prize.

By then the price of transistors had fallen from their 1953 level of $21 each to $1.50 and Shockley had left Bell. He moved to California and established in his home town of Palo Alto, at the seaward end of the Santa Clara Valley, the first monument to the new industrial age – a company called Shockley Semiconductor Laboratory. Though little has been heard of the firm since, there is a good case for arguing that Shockley Semiconductor was the most seminal company of all time.

Technospasm

When something really new like the transistor emerges from science, it faces both ignorance and suspicion; ignorance on the part of those companies and ultimately those consumers who will derive benefit from the invention and suspicion on the part of those companies whose livelihoods are threatened by it.

That suspicion and unease were in order amongst suppliers is illustrated by what happened to the US electronic components industry during the two decades following the appearance of the transistor. In 1955 the ten leading manufacturers of thermionic valves (tubes) were, in order of size, RCA, Sylvania, GE, Raytheon, Westinghouse, Amperex, National Video, Ranland, Eimac and Lansdale Tube. Of these only RCA managed to stay in the mass components business during the next two decades though it had slipped from top of the tube table to number eight in the integrated circuit rankings by 1975.

It was not just a question of getting into transistors early; you had to stay in too. Most of the leading transistor-makers in 1955, when the market was in its infancy, had disappeared from the integrated circuit rankings twenty years later. Survivors included Texas Instruments (which later achieved dominance in the field, boosting its 1955 transistor ranking of fifth to first place in the 1975 IC league table), RCA and Motorola. Transistor pioneers who dropped out of the race included Hughes, Transitron, Philco, Sylvania, Westinghouse and Clevite. New names to appear were Fairchild, National Semiconductor, Intel, Rockwell, General Instruments, Signetics and AMI.

Ignorance on the part of consumers and users delays things but by definition such ignorance cannot deny an important invention its due forever because it will only be regarded as important if it eventually overcomes this ignorance. In the case of the transistor the delay was the best part of a decade. The speed of the new component's market penetration is well mapped by what happened to the US radio market during the period.

In the early 1960s the situation in the radio market appeared to be pretty straightforward. Sales had been rising quite steadily since the war but lately the growth rate had begun to level off; the market seemed poised to settle down at a sales level of about 8 million units a year. It was clear what had happened. The radio market had gone 'ex growth' in America for the simple reason that every household in the country that was likely to want one now had a radio. Sales of 8 million units a year merely represented replacement demand.

The transistor changed all that. Semiconductor amplifiers made radios much more reliable (the thermionic valve was expensive and notoriously prone to failure), cheaper to run, smaller and much less costly to produce. Taken together these quantitative changes added up to an important qualitative change. Though the 'tranny' radio performed the same function as the old tube-driven wireless, the new technology had endowed it with such portability and economy that it was abruptly suitable for a much wider range of uses and users.

When the first transistor radios began to appear on the market some one-and-a-half decades after Shockley's initial breakthrough, demand for radios exhibited a dramatically increased vitality. Sales quickly leapt upwards from the plateau they had reached during the early years of the decade and by the late 1960s they were averaging 30 million units a year. Once again, it was clear what had happened. Radios, from being by their nature a one-per-household product, had become, entirely because of the advent of the transistor, a one-per-person product.

This is one example of how technological advance can change the nature of a familiar product without changing its function. Another, more recent, example of the phenomenon is what happened to the computer market when Clive Sinclair launched his £100, ZX80 personal computer which was to be succeeded, within a year, by the more powerful, £70 machine, the ZX81.

Corporate fission

While Shockley's invention was bringing about a sea change in the consumer durables market, the company he set up in Palo Alto (it was the world's first 'concept' company), was setting the scene for a no less significant sea change in the business world. Shockley was one of the first to realise that in the fast-moving world of electronics, a world of which he was the co-founder, the key to success was not strong financial backing or lavishly equipped laboratories, but pure brainpower. Shockley became a head-hunter and, knowing the infant industry as well as he did, he hunted skilfully.

Among those who set out at Shockley's invitation from the east coast for the sunny climes of California was MIT-graduate Bob Noyce. At the time Noyce had been working for Philco, a company that had already begun to make a mark with its electrochemical etching process, the full significance of which would become apparent later.

But, having acquired a taste for the region and an appreciation of the approach Shockley had adopted towards the semiconductor market, Noyce left the company in 1957 only a year after he had arrived. He took another seven of Shockley's bright young men with him and together they set up Fairchild Semiconductor under the wing of the Fairchild Camera company. They represented a prodigious concentration of talent. They brought with them knowledge of two techniques: 'etching', with which Noyce had come into contact at Philco, and 'diffusion'.

This was two-thirds of the technical base from which the Integrated Circuit (IC) evolved. The final piece of the jigsaw was the 'planar' process developed by one of Fairchild's own scientists, Dr Jean Hoerni. Noyce put the three together and by 1959 had come up with the blueprint for an IC. Whether he should be credited with the invention of the IC is still a matter of debate for in February 1959, unbeknown to Noyce, Texas Instruments (TI) had filed a patent application for ICs designed by Jack Kilby. (For the benefit of patriots it may be worth noting that Professor G. W. A. Dummer of the Royal Radar Establishment, Malvern, England is often credited, even by Americans, with the distinction of being the first person to suggest the idea of the Integrated Circuit.) Kilby had joined TI in 1958, having become frustrated by the unwillingness of former employer, the radio and TV components supplier, Centralab, to devote resources to the miniaturisation of circuits. Amongst the scientists and engineers, circuit miniaturisation was THE project at the time.

A number of approaches had been tried. The National Bureau of Standards set up what came to be known as 'Project Tinkertoy' which was an attempt to package the various components into a standard, close-packing shape (as opposed to the conventional cylindrical shape). Another stab at miniaturisation was the so-called 'molecular engineering' route which, following the example set by the transistor, was an attempt to discover new materials out of which much smaller versions of electronic components could be made. At the time of Kilby's arrival, TI itself was working on an approach quite similar to 'Project Tinkertoy' known as the Micro-module. The idea was to make each component exactly the same size and shape and then to stack them all on top of each other in a component tower, the various strata being connected to each other by wires running up the sides of the stack.

Kilby's solution was much more elegant than any of these other ingenious approaches to miniaturisation. He decided to make all types of component, resistors, capacitors, transistors, etc. out of a single block of silicon. The first ICs were demonstrated within TI in 1958. The work was published when patent applications were filed the following year. Once again, the rest of the world was at first sceptical of the product, in some ways justifiably so. In retrospect though, the IC caught on quickly enough. Over the next two decades the packing density of circuits rose from 1 to 100,000 components. The scale of integration is still a long way from its theoretical limits.

'Demand pull' from the US space programme and from the military was important in the early years, but throughout there has been a strong element of 'technology push' as the electronics engineers themselves have single-mindedly pursued the goal of doing more and more with less and less. Buckminster Fuller called this process 'ephemeralisation' and suggested that doing more with less is a general feature of technological advance, not confined solely to electronics.

That may be so but with electronics there have been two important technological pressures that have hurried the process of 'ephemeralisation' along – first, the larger the scale of integration, i.e. the more components to a single chip, the faster the circuit works; second, the smaller the chip, the higher the 'yield' of good chips on a single wafer of silicon. No silicon crystal is flawless. This means that the more chips there are on a single wafer, the greater the number that avoid the flaws.

As the purely technical miniaturisation drama unfolded, a parallel evolution – equally unprecedented – was taking place in the corporate arrangements of the semiconductor industry.

Shockley's departure from Bell and Noyce's subsequent desertion of Shockley were precursors of the electronics company chain-reaction. At just about the time TI and Fairchild were achieving their simultaneous IC breakthrough, Fairchild itself began to break-up. First to leave to set up the firstborn of what was quickly to become a large family of 'Fairchildren' was the general manager Noyce had hired when he led his fellow defectors away from Shockley.

Others followed his example and when those third-generation companies began to succeed, they too budded off to form fourth-generation firms. Soon the whole of the Santa Clara Valley was littered with small silicon chip companies busily at work trying to keep their noses ahead of their cousins. Noyce has estimated that between the time the IC appeared at the end of the 1950s to the birth of the microprocessor in 1971, about 100 new companies were formed to produce semiconductor devices. All of them can trace their origins back more or less directly to Fairchild and then to Shockley Semiconductor itself.

The budding off and the race to keep in front is still going on – it is unclear whether the chain reaction process has an end.

Meanwhile, back at Fairchild Semiconductor, Noyce himself was undergoing the metamorphosis which was to transform him from a scientist into a scientist/entrepreneur. When his general manager left to form his own company, Noyce took over his job and found he enjoyed the work. He and his close friend and colleague Dr Gordon Moore built up the company steadily over the ensuing decade. However, by the late 1960s Noyce was beginning to find the fact that the company he had founded and developed was a subsidiary of Fairchild Camera increasingly irksome. So in the end he and Moore left also to found their own company, Intel.

It was to be a different sort of operation. Noyce had learned from his experiences at Fairchild. Intel was not to be a one-man band; key employees were to be given a 'piece of the action'. One of the key employees turned out to be Ted Hoff, who was to become the co-inventor of the microprocessor. Once again TI was the other claimant to the discovery and once again TI did the patenting. But it was Intel which launched the first microprocessor in 1971.

Integrating the integrated

The invention of the microprocessor was inevitable. There was a hunger for it in the industry just as the high cost and poor reliability of the valve had represented a hunger for something like the transistor and just as the high cost and time-consuming construction of circuits using discrete components had represented a hunger for something like the integrated circuit.

The problem bred by the IC was that each circuit, however densely packed with components, could only fulfil one particular task. The solution was strikingly simple. If you could solve the discrete component problem by putting all the components on a single chip, why not solve the problem of the IC's limitations by putting all the circuits on a single chip?

Less than two years after joining Intel in 1969, Stanford University graduate Ted Hoff found himself working on a project Intel had taken on for the Japanese calculator group, Busicom. Busicom had designed a set of calculator chips and wanted Intel to make them. The logic circuit was spread around eleven ICs and linking that lot together looked to Hoff like a daunting task. Hoff thought about it and while thinking he was mindful of his boss Bob Noyce's decision to take a gamble with densely packed memory chips – a gamble that by then looked as if it was going to pay off for Intel.

Hoff reasoned that he could simplify the Japanese design greatly if he could get all the logic from the eleven chips together on a single IC memory chip. He also realised, and this was the key, that any chip that could store data could also store a program. He ended up with a logic circuit nestled in the middle of an Intel memory chip.

The device worked, and overnight the semiconductor industry became a vigorous new member of the computer industry. At the same time the microprocessor hugely extended the range of computer applications by achieving a quantum jump downwards in computer hardware costs. Hoff's breakthrough was a dream start for Intel, and such were the management skills and personal charisma of Noyce and Moore that Intel managed to hang on to a sufficient number of its key employees to establish itself as the world's leading manufacturer of microprocessors. At the start, the Noyce and Moore goal was to achieve sales of $100 million a year within ten years. In the event, they did rather better than that – sales in the tenth year were around the $400 million mark.

But as our new company model might have predicted, Intel was already experiencing growing pains by the late 1970s. Noyce and Moore recognised them for what they were in good time. They decided to split the company into five autonomous divisions. They also created, university-style, the job of 'research fellow' – a position which has since become quite common in the California high-technology companies. The incumbents, who have more or less complete freedom to do what they like, are sometimes called 'outside contributors'. Intel's first research fellow was Ted Hoff.

However, even such enlightened growth management was insufficient, in the end, to contain completely the disintegrative pressures we have been discussing.

Early in 1981 a group of key Intel employees spun off to form Seeq Technology. Intel reacted by slapping a law-suit on them, seeking to prevent the new company from using Intel technology. Two years later, early in 1983, just after a cash-starved Intel had raised $250 million by selling 12 per cent of itself to the mighty IBM, 17 key technical employees from the subsystems division in Oregon left to form Sequel Computer Systems.

At Intel's annual meeting in April, 1983, chairman Gordon Moore rapped the defectors on the knuckles. Barely fourteen years after he and Bob Noyce had left Fairchild Semiconductor to form Intel, Moore said that any manager who took away and used Intel technology or who secretly lured employees away was violating his legal responsibilities and was being clearly unethical. George Orwell would have loved it.

Gene-machining

The intellectual event that precipitated the biotechnological revolution began far away in Cambridge, England, but like microelectronics it finally grounded in California.

It all started with the discovery of the structure of genes in 1953 by the American, Dr James Watson and by the Englishman, Professor Francis Crick. Their discovery was a classic example of the 'first past the post' form of competition which is the scientific equivalent of price competition in business.

Crick and Watson were racing against a number of teams, all of which were convinced that the cracking of the genetic code would turn out to be a discovery of historic importance. It was this instinct, shared with the Linus Pauling team working at the California Institute of Technology and with the Maurice Wilkins, Rosemary Franklin crystallography partnership in London, which was the real inspiration.

For the genetic code, when cracked, might easily have turned out to be entirely trivial – a quite arbitrary mechanism for transferring biochemical information. In the event the instincts of the genetic researchers proved to be strikingly sound. The publication of the Watson–Crick 'double-helix' model of the genetic code, for which Crick, Watson and Wilkins shared a Nobel Prize in 1962, was positively bursting with significance. The code was elegantly simple, comprising just four varieties of deoxyribonucleic acid (DNA), and the intertwining of the two strands immediately suggested a mechanism for evolution.

But even more important than the biochemical corroboration of Charles Darwin's ideas was the clue the double-helix offered to the unravelling of the secrets of inheritance; how the characteristics of one generation are passed on to the next. For if the DNA structure determined ontogeny (the development of the individual foetus to maturity), then in theory a new life form could be created in the laboratory. And so it proved. The idea was first seriously proposed by Dr Peter Lobban in a short paper for an alternative PhD thesis submitted to his supervisor Dr Dale Kaiser at Stanford University, California.

Lobban did not win a Nobel Prize for his work. Another Stanford team, Professor Paul Berg and Dr David Jackson, began working on the project independently and they finished first. Both teams kept in touch throughout the research and Berg actually suggested at one time that they should publish jointly. Kaiser advised Lobban against joint publication and in 1980 Berg was awarded a Nobel Prize.

Subsequently the genetic engineering techniques developed by Lobban and Berg were greatly improved by two other Californian scientists, Professor Stanley Cohen and Professor Herbert Boyer. Their work was not so pioneering but it was very practical – it made gene-splicing easier and quicker which in business terms means cheaper.

In 1976 Boyer joined up with the entrepreneur Robert A. Swanson to form a company called Genentech. Four years later, with a string of scientific successes behind them, Boyer and Swanson floated the company on the stock market. The shares were offered for sale at $30 apiece. On the first day of dealings they rocketed to $80 giving Genentech a market value of almost $600 million.

The Genentech flotation, which has since been followed by a number of equally dramatic biotechnology share issues, marked the beginning of the biotechnology explosion. In terms of business economics biotechnology looks like being lesson two in the new theory of the firm.

California in England?

These brief reviews of developments in microelectronics and biotechnology give some indication of the impact on the business establishment of rapidly advancing technology. Men like Shockley, Noyce and Boyer are early examples of the new breed of business animal which I call the 'scientist/entrepreneur'.

Biotechnology is not so far down the road as microelectronics yet, but it is moving fast. Other small companies like Biogen, Cetus and Genex have already established the tradition of the independent brainpower company competing successfully with the established giants in the biochemical and pharmaceutical industries.

The question that will be addressed in the next section is whether similar tendencies are evident in Britain. For a number of reasons which will be dealt with later we should not expect such developments to be quite so visible here as they are in America. This is already an important weakness of the British system because visible success acts as an encouragement for others. The fundamental question though is whether companies like Intel and Genentech are emerging in Britain, visible or not.

If they are, and the next seven chapters are designed to show that this is indeed the case, then the conventional view of the British economy as being in the throes of a chronic process of 'de-industrialisation' needs to be modified.

The significance of the small, high-technology companies is out of all proportion to their as-yet-modest contribution to Britain's total national output. They represent the leading-edge of structural change, and in the long term the health and vigour of these young shoots now emerging from the corporate undergrowth are *much* more important than the ailments that beset the larger, more well-established companies.

The British economy is seldom viewed in this way. The conventional wisdom is that we are in deep trouble here because our industrial establishment is in poor shape. We tend to look at our economy through whatever is the opposite of rose-coloured spectacles. We see the inefficient and the dilapidated; the subsidised and the sub-competitive; the declining, the dying and the dead.

We accept this morbid view not because it is all there is to see but because, just as it was with the death throes of the dinosaurs millions of years ago, this is where the real drama appears to be. The closure of a shipyard or a steel mill can rip the heart out of a community and the billions of pounds spent on subsidies for our ailing motor industry visibly impoverish all of us. We see, hear and feel the process of de-industrialisation taking place all around us. The parallel process of re-industrialisation is, for the time being, below the threshold of normal perception.

To an outside observer the British economy, like the family of dinosaurs 65 million years ago, might appear to be standing on the brink of calamity. The old industrial empires are falling, unemployment is rising to dizzy heights, competition from abroad seems mostly unbeatable; only our oil stands between us and national destitution.

But an outsider observer who had witnessed the end of the dinosaurs and had feared as a consequence for life itself would have learned not to be too hasty. He would narrow his focus and would begin searching the undergrowth of industry for the equivalent of the small, furry, warm-blooded creatures, quick and lively, who, aeons ago, were preparing to inherit the Earth.

PART II

The corporate undergrowth

Introduction

The purpose of the seven chapters in Part II, each of which describes the development of a high-technology British company, is to shed some light on the sort of things that are going on in our corporate undergrowth. My hope is that this case study approach, in addition to providing the basis for a number of policy prescriptions which will be outlined in chapter 10, may also offer a few clues about the direction in which corporate evolution is progressing.

I have argued in Part I that giant companies are on the brink of extinction, but I have so far offered only a very general description of the sort of companies that will replace them. They will be smaller, but what else will they be? An evolutionary biologist might begin his search for answers to this question by investigating in some detail the early life of a number of companies.

Mindful of the correspondence that has been found between the evolution of species and the development of individual members of each species – a correspondence between 'phylogeny' and 'ontogeny' – he would study the embryos of companies in the hope of finding characteristics which disappear in later life.

In addition to the so-called 'law of recapitulation' popularised by the German naturalist Ernst Haeckel, which states that 'ontogeny recapitulates philogeny' – that each creature recapitulates the stages of its species' evolution in its developing embryo –

there is believed to be another, and for our purposes a more intriguing, correspondence between evolution and development. It is known as 'neoteny' (literally, 'holding youth') and was first proposed in the 1920s by the Dutch anatomist Louis Bolk. It is also known as the theory of 'foetalisation'. Bolk's idea was that many evolutionary progressions, from ape to man for example, can be understood in terms of the retardation of foetal development. In support of his theory he adduced a long list of features that human beings share with the immature but not the adult versions of other mammals.

Stephen Jay Gould, in his book *Ever Since Darwin*, lists some of Bolk's most important observations:

1 Our rounded, bulbous cranium, containing our large brain. Embryonic apes and monkeys have a similar cranium but, because their subsequent brain growth is much slower than ours, the cranial vault emerges lower and smaller in adults. Bolk suggested that we achieved our larger brains by retaining rapid foetal growth rates.

2 The human face, distinguished from those of other primates by a straight profile, small jaws and teeth and weak brow ridges, is very reminiscent of the face of the juvenile ape. The similarity fades as the ape's jaw accelerates its growth in relation to the rest of the skull, producing the adult's characteristic muzzle.

3 The 'foramen magnum', the hole in the mammalian skull from which the spinal cord emerges, is beneath the human skull pointing downwards as it is in the embryos of most mammals. This position is important because it means that when we are standing upright, we look forward. In other mammals the 'foramen magnum' rotates to a position behind the skull, pointing backwards, as the animal matures. This position is ideal for four-footed life.

Gould comments: 'The three morphological features most often cited as marks of humanity are our large brain, our small jaws and our upright posture. The retention of juvenile features may have played an important role in evolving all of them.' Whether neoteny is a sufficiently general idea to apply to economics and the corporate world is for the reader to decide. Conjecture along these lines is interesting, however.

We should regard the company or firm as an individual member of a species that is evolving in response to changes in the commercial environment. If we assume for the moment that the technological explosions that are taking place in the fields of electronics and biology are equivalent in some way to an ice age or to some other catastrophic change, then the idea of neoteny focusses attention on the embryos of the corporate species – the young, small companies that operate on the technological frontiers. If neoteny is applicable here, we should be able to catch glimpses of what tomorrow's mature companies will be like in today's juvenile companies.

It is not possible to pluck new corporate models, better adapted to a changed environment, out of thin air. The adaptations must come from a pre-existing pool of potential variation and by far the most important of such pools is that collection of embryonic qualities that have until now tended to disappear during maturation. The difficulty, of course, is to identify which of the juvenile qualities will actually be selected.

Anyone disposed to embark on a study of neoteny as it might apply to corporate evolution will have two main sources of data: the early lives of today's mature and successful companies, which are described in a number of corporate biographies, and the less accessible body of evidence about tomorrow's mature and successful companies, to which the following chapters make a small contribution. (I have tried to indicate in the text where I think neoteny might be at work).

I should emphasise that none of these seven stories is complete. They should be seen as segments of longer stories, the later chapters of which will unfold in the years ahead. The break point at which the segments end is the autumn of 1982.

I should also emphasise that none of these stories is entirely objective. Here and there, where they have involved other people and other organisations, I have attempted to confront the protagonist's views and recollections of events with those of others who were also involved.

For the most part though, the stories are my reconstruction of events recounted to me in a series of long interviews with the entrepreneurs concerned.

3
Dr David Murray and Sera-Lab

The story of David Murray as a man, living and working with other men and women, is almost ridiculously colourful. It lurches from the exotic to the tragic, from the absurd to the bizarre, all the while teetering on the brink of a lonely and dogged kind of heroism.

In comparison the story of David Murray as an entrepreneur is clinically straightforward. Aided by appropriate learning, luck and an extraordinary ability to spot opportunities, he has managed, from a standing start, and from a position on the outer edges of the technological mainstream, to steer his company into the vanguard of a new and vigorous industry.

He gives the lie to those who believe that inspiration is something that comes out of the blue, very rarely and only to young minds unburdened by the cares and responsibilities of adulthood. David Murray was 44 when he set up in business on his own, and now, at the age of 60 and on the brink of success, he seems lean and hungry. He was born in October 1922. He went to school at Hythe in Kent, then on to Dover College where he did well in English, Physics, Biology, Chemistry and French.

The war was on when he left school to join Ardente Acoustic Laboratories, peace-time manufacturers of massive deaf-aids which the hard-of-hearing had to carry around with them in large suitcases. By the time David arrived the company was supplying loud-hailers to the Ministry of Defence. Indeed

Ardente pioneered loud-hailer technology before Tannoy achieved its dominance of the market.

While at Ardente Murray invented the electric guitar. He cannibalised small electromagnets from telephone handsets, tuned them to each individual guitar string and connected them to a multichannel amplifier input. The device was first used by the well-known guitarist Roland Peachey (and his Royal Hawaiians). As we shall see, David Murray had connections in clubland.

In 1943 he volunteered for the Royal Air Force and was seconded to the Special Investigation Branch. Much of his work in the SIB was of the clandestine kind, involving frequent night trips across the Channel in small boats.

After the war David Murray decided to see the world and pick up some education on the way. He went to America where science tuition was good and qualifications were more speedily come by. He obtained a DSc in Biology and began preparations for a career in research. His chosen subject was genetics, which was about to enter one of its most gloriously creative periods culminating in 1953 with the publication of Crick and Watson's paper on the structure of the DNA molecule.

But then Dr Murray was whisked away from the thoughtful world of research to a glaringly different way of life. His father was the Percival Murray of Murray's Cabaret Club, the leading London night-spot where Jack Profumo met Christine Keeler. Murray the elder was ill and he begged his son to come home and help him with the business for a while. David consented. The routine seems exhausting. Murray would get into work at 11.00 a.m. and help with stock control, ordering and with preparations for the show in the evening. He would go home to change at 7.00 p.m. and then return to the club. He would get to bed at about 5.00 a.m.

But young David still found plenty of scope for his creative bent. He devised a new lighting system for the floorshow to overcome the problems associated with the basement club's 9-foot ceiling. It employed low voltage lights and was so successful that it was later marketed by Strand Electric. It is still being sold today. He also solved the problem of trailing microphone cables for the floorshow by inventing the radio microphone some four years before it became commercially available. Murray went on to develop the first solid state dimmer for strip lights and he also learned a thing or two about marketing. 'I soon realised', he recalls, 'that if a particular brand of cigars was selling slowly the simple answer was to double the price of the box – they would sell out overnight.' But despite the improvements, Murray's Club was running into problems.

When it opened in 1931 musicians worked for free, waiters and hat-check girls worked for tips and the head porter 'bought the door'. After the war, as society's conscience became more formalised, the economics of the club business began slowly to deteriorate. The emergence of the actors' union Equity and its counterpart amongst musicians, plus shops and catering legislation designed to protect the interests of a labour force too diffused to protect itself, all increased costs.

At the same time Percival Murray was indulging himself on the proceeds of the club with some extravagance. It became clear that something radical would have to be done if the club were to survive. David proposed that Murray's should buy the Beak Street building to strengthen its balance sheet and should then set about turning itself into London's most exclusive gaming club. Percival agreed and so David Murray began to prepare for a major diversification.

His first task was to learn all there was to know about gambling. He struck up a friendship with Frank Caparelli, a professional American gambler, who took him round all the London clubs, teaching him the conventions, styles and above all the odds. In the process Murray became no mean gambler himself. Having mastered the technical side, David started to lay the groundwork for the transformation proper. He persuaded Bob Barnett, then doing good business at the Curzon House Club in Mayfair, to come in as a partner, and he arranged the bank, complete with a financial syndicate to underwrite it. Everything was set to go.

Then Percival Murray took fright at what seemed to him to be an emerging challenge for dominance from his son. He squashed the project. From then on Murray's Cabaret Club was doomed. It struggled on for another eight years but finally went into liquidation with enormous debts in 1974. David Murray was long gone by then.

It was not just the gaming affair which caused the breach;

there was another, more personal, side to what turned out to be a permanent parting of the ways. Percival Murray disapproved deeply of his son's love affair with a girl called Lynette. David refused to give her up and so his father cut him off with the proverbial penny.

The couple thus found themselves out on the street with no job, no prospects and one grossly inappropriate asset – a 32-foot diesel-powered boat which had been David's pride and joy. The boat was sold for £12,000 and they began looking for somewhere to live and for something to do.

David would have liked to have taken up his academic career where it had been interrupted by his father's request for help for that 'short period' a decade previously. He knew it was impossible. He was 44 and his knowledge of a science that had been developing rapidly during his stint at the club was hopelessly out of date.

But even if he could take no active part in research, he still wanted to be close to it. By talking and listening he learned that laboratories were badly supplied with rabbits; biologists were always complaining about problems in the animal house and most of these problems were associated with rabbits. In 1968, if a research team wanted 60 rabbits of the same weight and sex they had to go to dealers and instead of ordering 60 rabbits they had to buy 80 or more to allow for an average mortality rate of 25 per cent. This was because dealers bought rabbits from a score or so of small breeders and though they bought the best they could find, they could never solve the problem of cross-infection.

Each rabbit herd has its own 'endemic pathogens'. When you mix different herds together as the dealers had to do to fill large research orders, they all start suffering from each other's pathogens. Diseases a particular stock has acquired resistance to become killers for others. It was this phenomenon which put paid to the Martians in the H. G. Wells science-fiction classic, *War of the Worlds*.

David Murray spotted an opportunity. He reasoned that if research orders could be filled from one large herd, the cross-infection problem would be eliminated. He could charge 25 per cent more per rabbit than the going rate and his customers would still be getting a bargain because of the minimal mortality rate. In addition he expected significant economies of scale in running a large herd. Lynette was good with small animals and she approved of the idea. They bought a tumbledown house called Parkfields near Crawley in Sussex and set about the two-year task of building up a rabbit herd.

First stop was the poultry show at Earl's Court in London. They came across the stand of a company called Wetley Abbey Livestock, which had on show a few cages of pretty little bunnies and some photographs of an imposing estate. The deal was that the customer paid 10 per cent down, got £5,000 worth of equipment and paid back the difference in rabbits. It seemed an ideal way to start so a few days later they drove up there. The set-up was as impressive as it had looked in the pictures; there were vans with the company's name on them, secretaries, telex machines, maps with pins stuck in them – all the trappings and appearance of a large company with an international scale of operations.

Murray was persuaded by some high-powered US-style salesmanship to part with £500 as a deposit for the position of Wetley's Sussex superintendent franchisee and for £5,000 worth of rabbit hutches which was to be delivered the following week. It was only after he had parted with the money that Murray's still rudimentary commercial antennae began twitching. He had nothing to go on but the company's catalogue. He rang the printer pretending to be connected with Wetley and was immediately subjected to a stream of invective about a long overdue bill. The cage manufacturers told the same story. It turned out later that all the vans were on the 'never never', that the signwriter had not been paid either and that the Earl's Court exhibition organisers were also waiting in vain for payment. The whole set-up was an elaborate fraud designed to part 'marks' from their deposit money.

Murray's response to these disclosures was to hire a van and drive straight up to Wetley. He arrived in mid-afternoon to find the place deserted. He broke into the shed where the cages were kept, dismantled £500 worth and began loading it. When he was approached by three 'heavies' he took pictures of them and threatened to sell the story to the *Sunday People*. The fraudsmen took fright and helped him load the van. The victory did not sustain the couple long. The next two years were a real struggle. There was never enough money. It got to the stage when they were thankful it was Sunday because writs were not served on Sundays.

The problem in the early years was to earn enough to keep going. The only way to do that was to sell a few animals for meat. Right at the beginning they had been promised 1 shilling per pound for rabbits by a local meat-processing company. When 12 months later Murray reckoned he could spare 30 rabbits from the breeding herd he rang the company up. He was offered 10 pence per pound, take it or leave it. He left it, feeling betrayed and profoundly depressed.

That was when the luck which Murray believes all entrepreneurs need from time to time began to make itself evident. Lynette suggested they drive around looking for other rabbit farms. It seemed a terribly long shot but there did not appear to be anything else to do. After a while they came across a large, old-fashioned rabbitry run by an unprepossessing-looking individual with string tied round his mackintosh.

Murray was not aware of it immediately, but this was an historic meeting. The man was Claud Goodchild, the doyen of rabbit dealers. He was the most prominent member of an industry which David Murray's company was both designed and destined to render extinct.

As Goodchild held up the precious rabbits by their ears to inspect them, Murray told himself he would accept nothing less than 4 shillings a head. After muttering a while, Goodchild said 'I'll give you 30 shillings a head and not a penny more'. Murray accepted the offer with as much of an appearance of reluctance as he could muster. The interim financing problem was solved. Goodchild was a regular buyer from Ranch Rabbits until the herd reached maturity 18 months later.

Goodchild's problem and that of other dealer/suppliers to the laboratory market was that they did not understand what the scientists needed. They knew nothing about autogenous pathogens and the importance of consistent quality. They just bought and sold rabbits. The scientists put up with the poor quality because, until David Murray's Ranch Rabbits came along, there was no alternative.

The first task when the herd matured in 1970 was to find buyers. The initial contact was with Doug Smith, chief purchasing officer for the Beechams laboratories at Brockham. Smith was impressed by the herd and by the idea behind it. He advised the couple not to sell cheap and they took his advice. From the very beginning Ranch Rabbit animals sold at twice the going price for laboratory rabbits which was then about £3 a head.

There were some bad moments just after the launch. Murray remembers feeling very depressed tramping around an annual conference of laboratory technicians, realising he had no idea who to talk to. Once again Lynette came to the rescue. She took him into the conference dining-room at lunch time, chose a likely table where half-a-dozen or so people were already seated, and they pulled up a couple of chairs. 'She was lovely', David Murray remembers, 'She charmed them all.'

Ranch Rabbits was established over that lunch.

And then, just before the company began to take off, Lynette died. Grief-stricken, Murray threw himself into work. For a long time after her death he regularly put in 18 hours a day, seven days a week. Between the years 1968 and 1976 he never had a holiday. The difference between a good business idea and a profitable company is often sheer hard work and so it was in this case.

David Murray is grateful for the support he received in those early days from Barclays Bank. He had been with Barclays during his years in London and when he felt the need for business banking services, it seemed natural to turn to his branch in Russell Square. The manager advised him to go to the East Grinstead branch, explaining that in farming communities branch managers had much more discretion than their more humble cousins in town. The East Grinstead manager Peter Foreman understood immediately what David Murray was trying to do with Ranch Rabbits and was extremely helpful. The growth of the company to the point where it was and remains the largest closed and accredited laboratory herd in the country was helped significantly by enlightened local banking. That Barclays was unwilling to follow Murray down other roads should not detract from the support and encouragement provided at the beginning.

One of the more irksome problems Murray encountered in

the normal, day-to-day running of Ranch Rabbits was the frequent last-minute cancellations or deferments of orders.

The reason invariably given by customers was that their animal houses were full to bursting with rabbits on long-term antiserum production. This is a common use of laboratory rabbits. The animals are injected with 'antigens' by the scientists and are then left to generate antiserum with their own body chemistry. Once generated the antisera are extracted from the blood with the help of a centrifuge.

The problem was that even with the high and consistent quality of Murray's rabbits, it was never possible to predict beforehand how long it would take for each rabbit to develop a sufficient strength or 'titre' (pronounced 'teeter') of antiserum. This variability was one of a number of uncontrollable factors in antiserum production which made the process imprecise and which consequently made the diagnostic sciences, the principal users of antisera, fundamentally inaccurate.

If there is a single theme to David Murray's business career from the time he established Ranch Rabbits in 1967 to the present, it is a continuous attempt to improve the precision and accuracy of the biochemical tools he supplies to the research market. And if there is a single feature which characterises the Murray strain of entrepreneurship, it is the man's ability to see the opportunities that lie embedded in problems.

Others might have tackled the order cancellations by trying to work out better scheduling systems. It would never have occurred to them to examine the time-honoured demarcation lines dividing the functions of the laboratory rabbit supplier from those of the user. But David Murray suffers, as do most entrepreneurs, from an inability to take things for granted.

Aided and encouraged by his friend Ron Chambers, Chief Technician of the Research Division at Queen Victoria Hospital, he decided to form a new company in 1971 called Sera-Lab. Ron Chambers, a loyal Ranch Rabbits customer and a man well-versed in the problems of maintaining animal houses and raising antisera, became a director and the holder of a 5 per cent equity stake. Murray and Chambers reasoned that since rabbit ordering difficulties were caused by antisera-raising problems, it might help if Murray did the antisera side too, using the customer's antigens and instructions (or 'protocols').

Murray describes the diversification like this: 'I started Sera-Lab originally as a service company to Ranch Rabbits and we raised antisera in our rabbits using clients' own antigens. When somebody wanted to put an order forward, I proposed instead that they sent me the antigen and the protocol, we carried out the innoculations, sent test bleeds for the client's approval and we prepared and supplied them with the antiserum.'

There were clear benefits for both sides. Customers no longer had to bother with the chore of raising antisera and in some cases they actually felt able to close down their animal houses altogether. The Maidstone Health Authority was the first to take this step and others followed. From Murray's point of view, the new arrangement made rabbit breeding much more profitable. He sold the antiserum for £1 per millilitre. One rabbit could produce about 25ml of antiserum, so its value, which was about £6 in those days, became £25 when used for antiserum production. The extra costs involved were mostly time. All that was needed were regular supplies of hypodermic needles and syringes, a centrifuge and a large refrigerator.

The response to the first mail shot was mixed. Some saw the sense of the idea straight away, but there were patches of resistance. Many biologists pride themselves on their antisera-raising technique and, though it may be only a minor part of their work, they regard it as an important part of the research ritual which they are reluctant to give up.

Even so Sera-Lab prospered. The service was enlarged to include other animals such as goats, sheep and guinea pigs. Murray and his staff became antisera experts. Each research laboratory had tended to evolve its own antisera-raising style. Now, for the first time, much of this lore was gathered together in one place, where it could be compared.

Whenever customers supplied sufficient quantities of antigen, Sera-Lab would experiment, varying protocols, using differing strains of rabbits, applying a number of antigen amplifiers ('adjuvants') and generally tinkering around. Results were often improved by such experimentation and customers were informed of the refinements.

Largely through the activities of Sera-Lab, the raising of antisera became a more efficient and scientific activity in Britain during the early 1970s. But the market ran out of steam, reaching a plateau in 1974 where it has stayed ever since. Competitors have emerged, such as the Unilever subsidiary Seward Laboratories, and there has been an increasing trend of late for large customers to take antisera production back 'in house'.

Murray, however, was not ready to go ex-growth just yet. From being an innovative rabbit breeder he had become, almost by accident, a part of the pharmaceuticals industry. People were used now to buying vials of liquid from him as well as animals, and some had become quite complimentary about the odd batches of non-immune serum he supplied by special order. These compliments puzzled Murray because there is nothing very difficult about producing serum. You draw whole blood from animals, allow it to clot naturally leaving the red cells clumped together at the bottom of the container and then you draw off the 'supernatant' at the top. Then it's into the centrifuge with it and after that you pour off the clear serum. You filter it to 0.2 micrometres, immediately freeze it at –20°C and deliver it in frozen state.

Why should Sera-Lab be so much better at this relatively simple task than the then leading suppliers of non-immune serum? Murray decided to investigate.

He found that because the serum market was large, the two main suppliers were taking short cuts. Instead of allowing the whole blood to clot naturally, they were 'defibrinating' it, which is not so effective, and in addition they were not using a centrifuge but rather a separation technique designed for the dairy industry to separate cream from milk. Finally, they were holding large stocks of raw serum prior to filtration which, despite storage at low temperature, resulted in a slow build-up of tiny, unfilterable bacteriophages in the serum.

So Murray decided to enter this market too. Sera-Lab's first catalogue was issued in 1976. It offered high-quality animal sera and a specialist range of antisera. The possibility of yet another diversification presented itself almost immediately. Murray quickly found that by volume, 90 per cent of the serum market was accounted for by foetal calf serum. The substance is widely used as an additive in tissue culture where a foetal serum is essential. Any other kind would introduce antibodies to the culture medium which could inhibit the growth of the cell line.

But there is an important constraint on the foetal calf serum market. The animal health authorities of various countries including Britain are keen to prevent the spread of livestock epidemics like rinderpest and foot-and-mouth disease. Since these are virus diseases it is virtually impossible to filter them out. There is therefore a ban in Britain on the import of serum from countries where these crippling diseases are endemic.

Australia has never been plagued by foot-and-mouth, blue tongue and the other killer cattle diseases, and is thus the world's main exporter of foetal calf serum. Since apparently pregnant cows were not slaughtered in Britain, David Murray flew to Australia to secure his supplies. Murray found, much to his disappointment, that all Australian sources of foetal calf serum were tied up by the two companies he had just set up in opposition to in the UK serum market. He was disturbed somewhat by the low hygienic standards of Australian collection methods, but since all supplies were spoken for this was no more than a critical scientific observation by an experienced serum supplier more mindful than most about the importance of hygiene and purity.

But Murray was not finished yet. He decided he would first check what everyone had told him about British slaughtering practices; that pregnant cows were simply never slaughtered here; that when cows grew old they always went to the knacker's yard; that pregnancy was only induced by artificial insemination or by arrangement with a stud bull with a view to keeping the calf. He found that it had all been true once upon a time, but that it was not any more.

Unbeknown to other serum producers, changes in animal husbandry, coupled with British membership of the European Community, had begun to generate the means for establishing a domestic supply of foetal calf serum. When we joined the EEC, abattoirs discovered that there was a substantial demand, especially in France and Belgium, for cow meat as opposed to steer meat. This gave the farmer the financial incentive to send cows in prime condition for slaughter. The British farmers had also discovered that allowing a young bull to run freely in the fields with the dairy herd, servicing the cows regularly and indiscriminately, improved milk yields and made the cows more placid.

The result of these changes was that when David Murray investigated UK abattoirs, he found that about 10 per cent of all cows sent for slaughter were pregnant. He had found his supply of foetal calves. He quickly developed a new, aseptic 'exsanguination' method using cardiac punctures and added to Sera-Lab's catalogue fresh, high-quality foetal calf serum. But there were a number of unexpected hurdles to clear before Sera-Lab would begin to reap the full benefit of the foetal calf serum venture.

A couple of years earlier Murray had bought a small rabbit herd to protect his market position. He disbanded it, but kept on the breeder as his rabbit manager so that he would have more time to devote to Sera-Lab. The rabbit manager had a pleasant but rather inefficient assistant to whom Murray gave the job of collecting foetal calf serum from a local abattoir where the pilot project was being carried out. After a while the supplies of serum began to drop alarmingly. According to the abattoir manager the reduction had nothing to do with the number of pregnant cows being slaughtered. So Murray hired a couple of private detectives to find out what was afoot. It emerged that the assistant, in collaboration with the rabbit manager, was selling serum on his own account to a Sera-Lab competitor. Murray sacked them both on the spot.

A couple of weeks later rabbit sales began to take a dive for no accountable reason. A customer rang to inquire whether Murray was aware a rumour was circulating that Ranch Rabbits was not the closed, accredited herd it made itself out to be and that Murray was actually a dealer of the Claud Goodchild variety.

And if that was not enough, it turned out that the Inland Revenue had been 'tipped off' that Murray was an ex-gangster whose business affairs would not bear close investigation. A similar story had been told to the Crawley police and Murray received several visits from CID people, whose suspicions were further aroused by a number of drawings by Dr Stephen Ward that hung in Parkfields. It will be remembered that Dr Stephen Ward had featured in the Profumo scandal a decade or so earlier. He had been Murray's osteopath during the night-club era.

Fortunately Murray had made other contacts during those

years, amongst them a number of police officers who had since become quite senior. A phone call to one of them quickly put a stop to the investigation by the Crawley police. The Inland Revenue was not so easily put off. Murray's auditors say that since 1976 his have been the most closely investigated accounts they have ever handled. No less than eleven tax inspectors have embarked on the trail of the ex-gangster through his business affairs. The investigation was not finally concluded until 1981.

There have been other incidents too.

When Murray was in Greece in 1976, taking his first holiday since founding Ranch Rabbits nine years previously, he received a cable informing him that two of his senior staff, one of whom was a PhD scientist, had disappeared. Shortly after his return a new company, selling very similar products, emerged on the scene. The two directors were his ex-employees. To add insult to injury he began to receive bills made out to the new company. The Board of Trade mounted an investigation and the two men ended up in court.

Soon after the foetal calf serum business began to take off a whispering campaign against Sera-Lab was mounted by one of Murray's American competitors, suggesting the company was obtaining its serum from slaughters associated with brucellosis eradication schemes. Murray wrote to the company concerned threatening legal action and the rumours died out.

A price-war followed which Sera-Lab won comfortably because of its lower costs. Then the 'enemy' began to get tough. Attempts were made, through another company, to deny Murray access to his supplies of foetal calves. They were successful. Murray lost one of his largest abattoir suppliers and watched helplessly as the price of foetal calves moved against him. In the end, the entrepreneur who was acting on behalf of Sera-Lab's competitor rang Murray up, told him of the plot and offered to change sides. It had been touch and go for a while, but in the end the Murray luck held good.

The most striking example of David Murray's entrepreneurial quality is his immediate recognition of the commercial significance of 'monoclonal antibodies' (MABs). In some ways he was favourably placed to make this inspired leap. His mind was prepared. He had a good working knowledge of the subject, long experience in supplying the research market and an appreciation of the speed with which biology and biochemistry were developing.

And as we have seen, all the entrepreneurial initiatives he had taken in his career to date had been inspired in one way or another by the recognition that there was always a ready market for research reagents of a higher quality. He had never been wholly satisfied with his own products, good though they were in relation to the competition's.

The first Kohler and Milstein paper on MABs appeared in the science journal *Nature* (no. 256: pp. 495–7) in late 1975. Murray read it a few months later. He described to me the impression it made on him: 'I knew this must be the way forward. Here was, for the first time, a method of raising extremely avid, high titre and absolutely pure antiserum with each batch identical to the previous one in every respect.'

Murray wrote to Dr Cesar Milstein, expressing admiration for his work and proposing that Sera-Lab should market the MABs Milstein and his team were producing at the Medical Research Council's Molecular Biology Laboratory in Cambridge. A month or so later Murray was in Cambridge on a sales trip to promote the recently introduced foetal calf serum. He was unaware at the time that Milstein had already become one of his customers.

On the off-chance of another sale, Murray knocked on the door of the molecular biology lab. He was invited to enter and found himself facing a small, dark man sitting at a desk piled high with an untidy mountain of papers. Murray introduced himself and launched into his sales pitch. He does not remember the exact words, but the conversation continued something like this: 'Oh, Dr Murray, I've been meaning to reply to your very interesting letter'; the man plunged his hand, apparently at random, into the paper mountain and pulled out a piece of paper adorned with the distinctive Sera-Lab logo.

'I like your proposal', he continued, 'I've been spending most of my time these last few months running downstairs to the refrigerator, thawing a vial, pouring out an aliquot [a fraction], packing it up in dry ice and posting the parcels all over the world to people who have read about my work.'

It was only then that David Murray realised he was talking to the great Cesar Milstein himself. The two men discussed Murray's proposal and Milstein promised to support the idea of a Sera-Lab MAB marketing operation. But ultimately it would be up to the MRC and to its statutory marketing agency, the National Research Development Corporation (NRDC). The MRC had no commercial links in those days and wanted none. Times were hard though. Public-spending cuts, particularly of research grants, were beginning to bite. The idea of earning royalty income from outside had its attractions.

In the end, thanks to the NRDC's lack of interest and to Milstein's support, a deal was struck. It was agreed that the MRC would initially supply MABs to Sera-Lab in the form of 'supernatant' and 'ascites', and that when Sera-Lab had built a laboratory complex to raise MABs on its own, it would receive the precious cell-lines, the 'hybrid-myelomas' or 'hybridomas' as they came to be called, from which MABs are raised. It was always made clear throughout the negotiations that the NRDC had, by charter, a prior right to any MRC-funded inventions.

'I realised', Murray recalls, 'that one day soon the NRDC must wake up to the potential of what it had discarded and that my priority must therefore be to enter into similar contractual arrangements with other monoclonal research groups as soon as they appeared, to fund and collaborate with such groups and finally, of course, to carry out "in house" research for the more commercially viable cell lines.'

But the MAB opportunity could hardly have come at a worse time. The rest of Murray's business was falling apart. The foetal calf venture was consuming cash at an alarming rate just at the time when earnings from Ranch Rabbits were being affected by the arrival of a couple of aggressive competitors. Each of the new serum collection points in the abattoirs required equipment costing £8,000 and involved substantial running costs. In addition, the average customer required samples from three batches and took about five weeks to test them. This meant that large sums of money had to be tied up in stocks before any revenue was generated. And that was not all. The project had required the conversion of an existing cowshed into a fully equipped laboratory at an all-in cost of about £60,000.

Murray resorted to desperate measures to stem the cash outflow. He began selling batches of unfiltered serum at £10 a litre compared to the £30–40 a litre for the filtered stuff. It was no good. However he worked it, the figures just would not add up. It was clear that without bank help the business was doomed. Barclays took the view that Ranch Rabbits had been an original idea the viability of which had been quite easy to assess. They were not so sanguine about Sera-Lab. They argued that Murray was setting up in competition with established international companies with a firm grip on their markets. The bank feared that despite Sera-Lab's reputation for quality, the competition would squash it.

Things were so bad by then that it was faintly comical when, under the terms of the contract with the MRC, the time came for Sera-Lab to spend another £100,000 on a purpose-built MAB unit. David Murray had become convinced by then that he could not even keep his existing business afloat.

'Times were really very desperate', he relates. 'I had remortgaged my house to the hilt, I had sold every personal possession of value, I had raised a small sum – I think it was £9,000 – from COSIRA [the Council for Small Industries in Rural Areas], I even factored my Ranch Rabbits accounts which is a ghastly and expensive way of raising money. I remember in February 1978 sitting all night on the bank of a nearby lake, gazing over the water trying, unsuccessfully, to make myself accept the fact that Sera-Lab must be put into liquidation.'

But the morning after that lakeside vigil David Murray the gambler began to experience an absurdly prolonged and improbable run of luck.

Derek Barnett, a young accountant who had recently joined the company, suggested they should enter the MAB project in Thames Television's 'Time for Business' award for the most innovative business idea. The closing date for entries had by then long since passed, but Murray, clutching desperately at any straw he could find, phoned the organisers and asked them why Sera-Lab's entry to the competition had never been acknowledged. Thames were extremely apologetic and said that if they received a copy within 24 hours, they would try to include it in the programme.

The two men worked through the night and delivered the entry by hand on the following day, a Tuesday. On Wednesday Thames phoned to ask whether Murray could be at the studio on Thursday for that week's edition of *Time for Business.* On the following Thursday, during the final programme of the series,

Sera-Lab was declared the winner. The three judges were inventor and entrepreneur Nigel Vinson, an area manager from the Midland Bank, and Hugh Armstrong of Development Capital, the company which was supposed to be supplying the £150,000 award.

Vinson was very complimentary. He said he had been impressed by David Murray's ability to see a problem and to overcome it; the bank manager had no hesitation in saying that he would willingly back such a venture; Hugh Armstrong said nothing until after the programme. It was only then that Murray realised what the award consisted of. He was told that if he wanted the £150,000 he would have to surrender 30 per cent of the Sera-Lab equity and enter into loan agreements carrying what Murray later described as 'an excruciatingly high interest rate'.

The let-down was dramatic but short-lived, as Murray explained to me with his tongue fixed firmly in his cheek: 'Fortunately I did not have to accept this kind offer because, quite by coincidence, I got a phone call from Barclays the following day to say they had been thinking about Sera-Lab and they really felt they should do something to help.'

From that day to this, Barclays have been model bankers, provided always that they are supplied with the information they need.

Derek Barnett had taught David Murray a thing or two about banking psychology. When Murray first asked for a loan to finance the MAB project he had no prepared answers. When they asked him for sales projections all he could say was; 'I'm no crystal ball-gazer, I just think it's going to be fantastic.' That does not do with banks. As Barnett said, when you are dealing with something quite new you have to pluck figures out of the air if necessary, and then explain later why they were not quite right.

Shortly before the Thames competition, Murray had entered, as a last resort, into an arrangement with the Industrial and Commercial Finance Corporation (ICFC), the development capital organisation owned jointly by the clearing banks and the Bank of England. The money involved was nothing like enough, but it had given ICFC an option to acquire equity at a later stage. Thankfully Barclays insisted, with possibly a little pressure exercised through its holding in ICFC, on handling the whole package. The ICFC option was bought out for a modest sum. The new financing arrangement involved long- and short-term loans, good overdraft facilities and a little leasing finance obtained from Bowmaker. There was no request for equity.

The MAB unit was up and running in short order, hoisted into the laboratory complex, ready to run, by a huge crane. The MAB market proved more difficult to exploit profitably than David Murray had expected, but in the event that did not matter too much.

For the Murray run of luck was still delivering the cards in spades. The market for foetal calf serum, entry into which had almost broken Sera-Lab, was caught in the undertow of the biotechnology explosion. Prices soared from £35 a litre to £120 a litre and they stayed there for almost a year. All but Sera-Lab's long-term loans were repaid well ahead of the due dates, and there was enough money left over to finance a further extension of the laboratory. Foetal calf serum prices have fallen back substantially since. Scientists were shocked by the boom and have now begun to develop synthetic additives for tissue cultures. There is still money to be made out of the serum, and perhaps out of the new additives, but Sera-Lab's growth will be mostly monoclonal inspired from now on.

But the MAB market is not proving easy to develop. The arrival of something new, offering previously undreamed-of precision and economy, does not automatically mean that yesterday's methods get chucked out of the window. It does not matter to laboratory technicians how good or economical a test chemical is, just so long as it works and is easy to use.

So Murray has decided that the future for MABs in the diagnostic market is in what computer scientists would call 'user friendly' kits. He reckons he is a good year ahead of the competition in kit development, and he has been working closely with the Royal Free Hospital in London and with the influential National Institute for Standards in Biological Science.

There is still a great deal to do. Each MAB has different properties requiring different protocols, different temperatures, different storage methods, varying shelf-lives and even different sorts of glass or plastic for the containers.

David Murray would like to do a little less work himself now and bring in better scientific minds to the business if only on a royalty or consultancy basis. He particularly wants a new technical director but he is choosy now – he has had more than enough problems with picking the wrong staff. There are about forty people working at Parkfields, some twenty-five with Sera-Lab and the rest with Ranch Rabbits. Murray is setting up a share-participation scheme. He says, 'that's the only way to run a company in this day and age.'

The story of Sera-Lab sheds light on the interaction between small companies and the state, for in the end the qualified nature of Murray's understanding with the MRC became very important.

In 1980 the Advisory Council on Applied Research and Development (ACARD) published the Spinks Report on biotechnology in Britain. Spinks and his colleagues concluded that by and large British industry, with one or two honourable exceptions, had failed to respond to the challenge of recent biotechnological developments. They chided the NRDC for not patenting MAB technology* and they said that substantial sums of public money would need to be invested if Britain was to stand any chance of making good the ground already lost.

Celltech Ltd, conceived and created by Gerard Fairtlough and financed by private sector institutions and the National Enterprise Board, was one of the main results of the debate and deliberation inspired by the Spinks Report. Fairtlough was determined to get on equal terms with the foreign biotechnology

* It would be unfair to give the impression that the NRDC is the object of universal condemnation for its failure to patent MAB technology, and that the assignment of its rights in this area to Celltech was a punishment for such gross negligence.

The NRDC argues, and there are those within the MRC who agree, that it was not possible to patent such a general technology. Much better, according to the NRDC, to keep under wraps the cell-lines from which the MABs are grown.

This debate between those who believe secrecy is the best way to protect the commercial value of inventions and those who favour blanket patenting remains unresolved. It continues in all sorts of areas apart from biotechnology. The best that can be said now is that secrecy and patenting both have a role to play. It is a matter of horses for courses.

'concept' companies like Genentech and Biogen as soon as possible. He began to recruit talented scientists and to develop strengths in all the important areas including production technology, finance, management, marketing as well as pure science.

Most important from David Murray's point of view, Fairtlough requested and was granted what amounted to first-refusal rights to non-research MABs developed at the MRC's laboratories. He was aware that this arrangement, effectively an assignment to Celltech of rights that had belonged previously to the NRDC, would affect Sera-Lab. So Fairtlough offered to buy Murray's monoclonal operation for £70,000. Murray rejected the offer as he has so far rejected a dozen or so other takeover approaches. He felt Celltech's bid was derisory and merely reflected a wish to tidy up a loose end.

Fairtlough may not have known at the time that Murray's interest in MABs had extended beyond the research market into diagnostic kits, and in any case he felt that Celltech, which was from the outset a much larger and more substantially funded company, deserved to be the favoured national runner in the MAB race.

The MRC agreed. It had originally welcomed the arrangement with Sera-Lab because it relieved Milstein and others from the chore of producing and packaging samples. When Celltech came along – the creature of establishment concern about the lack of an integrated, science-led biotechnology company in Britain – it appeared to the MRC to be a more appropriate and, in some respects, a more capable vehicle for this purpose than Sera-Lab.

The MRC regards its five-year agreement with Celltech as an important advance over the previous relationships with the NRDC and with Sera-Lab. It is similar to the Sera-Lab agreement in that royalty payments go direct to the MRC rather than through the NRDC and it is, in the MRC's view, superior to the Sera-Lab agreement in that it imposes a number of additional obligations on Celltech. The MRC can, under certain circumstances, require Celltech to develop and market products and techniques that are not commercially viable, such as reagents for rare diseases. In addition, the MRC regards Celltech as better endowed scientifically than Sera-Lab, and thus a more suitable repository for the all-important cell-lines.

Sera-Lab is not excluded from the emergent MAB industry by Celltech's agreement with the MRC. Murray's contract still provides a trickle of MRC research reagents and there are now a number of other MAB sources dotted around the world. But it does seem a little unfair. After all, Murray was the pioneer. Both Celltech and the MRC would do well to deal gently with Sera-Lab; after all the MRC is a public body and Celltech is still 44 per cent state-owned.

I think in this case, at least, there was some justification for what has been done but Celltech will need to be successful to prove the point conclusively.

David Murray's great weakness as an entrepreneur has been his inability so far to recruit and keep good technical and scientific staff. This more than anything else has prevented him from building up the technological weight needed to take on companies like Genentech. If Sera-Lab had shown signs of shifting from a market-led growth to a science-led growth, then the MRC might have seen things differently and so perhaps might have Spinks.

Murray admits to the flaw while insisting it is much less evident now than it was. He says it was a reaction against the 'divide and rule' management style employed by his father at Murray's club. 'My father was a great manipulator of staff,' Murray remembers: 'he operated a "spy" system and used the information he gleaned to play one person off against another with brilliant but very cruel psychology.'

David believes this sort of thing is still quite common in UK organisations, but having experienced it he vowed never to use it himself. 'When I started my company,' he said, 'I wanted to believe that everybody who worked for me could be motivated purely by example and instruction coupled with what I hoped would be their own natural desire to show how good they were. I think I also believed that loyalty was an inherent quality in all of us given the right conditions in which to flourish. This may sound naive, but for everyone who has failed in this trust I can point to ten others who have confirmed my belief and overall I am confident that I run a happier ship than the vast majority of employers in this day and age.'

4
Steve Shirley and F International

Rank Xerox caused quite a stir in July 1982 when it introduced the idea of the 'networker' to Britain. Pressed for space in its London headquarters, the company invited 150 of its senior executives to become self-employed, working from home on part-time contracts. It was as if the office equipment company had lifted a corner of the curtain dividing the present from the future and had shown us a glimpse of a new world, made possible by modern technology, where the focus of work had shifted from the office block to the home.

But novel though the 'networker' idea appeared, it was not the first scheme of its kind. The pioneer of the high-technology cottage industry was Steve Shirley; the Rank Xerox networkers were following a trail she had blazed twenty years earlier.

Steve Shirley was born Vera Stephanie Buchthal on 16 September 1933 in Dortmund, West Germany. In 1939 she and her sister were brought to England by the Quakers to live with English foster parents near Birmingham.

She first went to the village school, but her foster parents soon became concerned about the broad 'Brummie' accent she acquired there, and they found a place for her at a private Roman Catholic convent school in Sutton Coldfield. She won a scholarship to a grammar school in Lichfield and then moved on to another in Oswestry. She says she 'loathed' school, but would have liked to have gone to university. It was not possible at the time, largely because the family was desperately short of money. Steve's father had been a high-powered lawyer in Germany before the War, but law does not travel well. A continental qualification means little in countries where Napoleon failed to impress his code on the legal system.

So at the age of 18 young Stephanie went to London, armed with a good general education, to look for a job. She was offered two, one at the Post Office research station at Dollis Hill and another at GEC's operation at Wembley. She says that one reason she chose Dollis Hill was the better security the job seemed to offer. She is amused now looking back on her younger self; serious, careful and averse to risks. Another attraction of the PO was the encouragement given to young technical staff to further their education. She quickly took advantage of this and enrolled for maths evening classes at the Sir John Cass College.

Her first task was to make good matriculation requirements in maths and physics which she did in a year. Four years later, with the help of day release from the PO, she obtained her BSc in mathematics. It was through evening classes that she first came into contact with computers. The only other student who finished the degree course was Bill Cameron, who was working at the GEC Hirst research centre. He told Steve of an interesting machine he was working with called HEC 4 and he invited her round to see it.

She was impressed. She met Bill Cameron's boss John Wensley and became keen to work more closely with what seemed to her to be a very interesting new technology. But she had no degree – not yet anyway – and in 1954 you needed a degree to work with computers.

Steve finds it curious now to look back at those very early days of computers when she was so impressed by machines which were really very primitive. 'I didn't realise then', she says, 'that computers were just a few years ahead of me.'

She was working with an even more primitive machine at the PO's technical department – the desk-top calculator. Unbeknown to most people at the time these push-button mechanical machines were about to become extinct. In skilled hands though, they were still capable of quite sophisticated arithmetic. Steve used them for statistics, probability and design problems and on more substantial projects like the premium bond system, ERNIE (Electronic Random Number Indicator Equipment).

She also investigated likely traffic patterns on transatlantic telephone cables and remembers being firmly rebuffed by the male marine establishment when she tried to wangle a trip on the cable-laying ship, *Monarch*. A particularly interesting period for her was a stint at the PO's research establishment, working on the design of futuristic electronic telephone exchanges for T. H. Flowers of Bletchley fame. She became aware that there had been something very special about the atmosphere at Bletchley – an aura of intellectual self-confidence and scientific boldness quite unknown to her.

The place is much on her mind these days because one of Steve's most absorbing pre-occupations at present is with what has come to be known as Knowledge Engineering or Artificial Intelligence.*

But back in the late 1950s, Steve's time with the PO was drawing to an end. She fell in love with Derek Shirley, a Post Office engineer working on 'wave-guides'. After a prolonged courtship they were married in November 1959. They are still

* Bletchley Park was the scene of the dramatic cracking of Germany's 'Enigma' code during the Second World War by a team of brilliant young mathematicians led by Alan M. Turing.

There are those who believe that Turing and his colleagues, including Donald Michie, now Professor Michie of the Department of Machine Intelligence and Perception at Edinburgh University, gave us the means to win the peace as well as helping us to win the war.

Had a succession of British governments not turned a deaf ear to Michie's pleas for state funding of machine intelligence research, Britain's position in this crucial area might have become well nigh impregnable. Perhaps even now, a quarter of a century after Alan Turing's tragic suicide, that position is still within our grasp.

An important lesson to learn from the Enigma affair is that when the British are presented with a goal of great importance on which to focus they can maintain prolonged and intense intellectual effort.

Goals like this tend to appear mostly in war time. The Japanese seem to be better at establishing challenging peace-time goals than we are and that is one reason why people like Donald Michie are so concerned about the threat to Britain's lead in Artificial Intelligence research posed by Japan's liberally-funded programme to develop so-called 'Fifth Generation Computers'.

Steve Shirley has advocated the establishment of a 'National Goal' for knowledge-engineering, designed to generate just that sort of focus and just that sort of effort.

married. They have a mentally handicapped son who is permanently hospitalised.

After the wedding Steve was keen to leave the PO. She and Derek both felt that it was not a good idea for husband and wife to work at the same place and anyway, she wanted to get to grips with computers now that she had her degree. She had done another year of evening classes by then, working towards an MSc in probability theory, but she gave it up when she realised that she lacked the ability to make an original contribution to mathematics.

She joined a new company called Computer Developments Limited, jointly owned by GEC and ICL's precursor, ICT. Her boss was the same John Wensley she had met at Wembley when she went, at Bill Cameron's invitation, to meet HEC 4. During her two years at CDL she helped to design the 1301 computer and became an adept programmer. She was one of the first of a new breed of software engineers. The job was highly skilled and very well paid by the standards of the day. When she left CDL she was earning £2,000 a year for a four-day week. It was her last job as an employee.

Steve Shirley recognises now that she was probably never the employee type. She regards herself as an entrepreneur and believes that all entrepreneurs, whether successes or failures, are virtually unemployable. 'They want to control their environment,' she explains, and they cannot do that if someone else is managing them.

There were a number of reasons for leaving CDL in August, 1962. She and Derek had been discussing plans for a family (she wanted five children) and convention was such in those days that eyebrows were raised at the working wife. People would mutter 'Doesn't Derek have a good enough job?' According to Steve, the decision to hand in her notice was taken during a meeting at work which brought home to her how irksome she found it to be an employee. The CDL staff were discussing pricing policies. Steve made a suggestion and was told 'This has got nothing to do with you, you're technical.' She was furious. 'That's it,' she thought, 'I'm off!'

She decided to go freelance. 'I thought I was so good', she recalls, 'that they'd all come flocking to my door.' Nothing happened for several months. She had let it be known she was in the market for work and she was by then fairly well known in the embryonic computer industry. She called her company Freelance Programmers.

The first job came three months later through a former CDL colleague who had by then also departed and was working for the Urwick Diebold management consultancy. Urwick Diebold, aware of the potential of the new technology, had set up a computer consultancy division. Steve was asked to design management controls for a data processing group.

By the time she finished the job she was eight-and-a-half months pregnant. Whenever she was asked during that first year how many people worked for Freelance Programmers, she used to say 'one and a bit'. After her son was born she lost interest in work for three months. She reckons it was nature's way of making sure the newborn baby received her undivided attention for a while.

Then she got an assignment from her old company, CDL. She found it quite easy and became involved in the business once more. It was about this time that she received an income tax demand based on her previous salary at CDL. The taxman wanted £600. She had only earned about £700 the whole year. 'I burst into tears', she recalls.

Freelance Programmers did not begin life with limited liability, but by 1964, when the work was beginning to trickle in, Steve began to get worried about the high cost of professional indemnity insurance. At the time she was working on a job for GEC connected with aircraft. The idea that something she had been responsible for might go wrong and cause the loss of life made her uneasy. With the help of a friend and a £15 'off-the-shelf' company Freelance Programmers became Freelance Programmers Limited (FPL).

Incorporation, though it was, in terms of what had to be done, a small and easy step to take, appears to Steve Shirley in retrospect to have been an important turning point. It was like laying an official foundation stone. The 'Ltd' somehow made the whole operation more credible, not only to her customers but also to herself. That she had not done it straight away as most people do meant that she had earned the status rather than merely claimed it. There is another reason why the year 1964 was important; it was the year FPL began to build up its 'panel' of homeworkers, the people who were and who remain the back-bone of the company. Until then, Steve had been alone; after that it became clear that there was potential for growth beyond what she could do herself.

She attributes the beginning of the panel build-up to the press coverage FPL began to attract. She regards one article that appeared in the *Guardian* on 31 January 1964 as having been of particular significance because of the publicity it gave to the idea behind her company. It was by Maureen Epstein and was head-lined 'Computer Women'.

Reading it now is like travelling back in technological time. It describes briefly what a computer is and explains what a programmer does. 'This is where the computer operator takes over. Her job is to tend the computer, to keep it fed with punched cards, and to see that its dials are correctly set.

'The programmer and the operator between them can replace a team of clerical staff. By buying a computer – current price between £80,000 and £500,000 – and by seeking expert help to programme and run it efficiently they can do away with all the day-to-day drudgery of the office, and even save money, as the computer can do several jobs as once.'

Mrs Epstein went on to enumerate the qualities required of operators and programmers; operators needed 'A' level maths, while programmers usually needed a degree. Most of all, though, it was a question of personality. The job required 'patience and tenacity, and a common-sense sort of logic. Much of the work is tedious, requiring great attention to detail, and this is where women usually score. Many find the job boring; others become fanatics about it.'

And then came the passage which gave FPL a boost along the road to success:

'One of the fanatics is Mrs Steve Shirley, of Chesham, Buckinghamshire. A mathematics graduate who considered herself "merely competent" at research mathematics, she has found in computer programming an outlet for her artistic talents in the working out of logical patterns. She describes the qualities required as "the ability to see both the wood and the trees."

'Now retired, with a young baby, she has found that computer programming, since it needs only a desk, a head, and paper and pencil, is a job that can be done at home between feeding the baby and washing nappies. She is hoping to interest other retired programmers in joining her in working on a free-lance basis.'

But with growth and the accumulation of the panel came cash problems. The work was coming in at a reasonable rate but Steve was not getting paid for it until after the jobs were finished. She was unaccustomed to the status of employer and her instinct was to pay panel contributors after they had completed their tasks. With the larger projects on which a number of people were involved, this sometimes meant that she was paying fees out before she received payment for the whole job. She decided to call in professional advice and turned to Urwick Diebold whose rates at the time were a stiff £150 a day.

The consultants sent round Kit Grindley who was to become a loyal friend and ally. He was both alarmed and impressed by what he found at FPL – so alarmed and so impressed that within a few days of meeting Steve Shirley he wrote her out a personal cheque for £500 to tide the company over its first cash-flow crisis.

He urged the young entrepreneur to adopt what came to be known as the principle of 'gearing' the timing of payments to panel members precisely to the timing of payments from customers. Steve did not like it but she saw the sense of it – gearing provided an automatic check on cash-flow and for many years it was an important feature of the management method.

Looking back, Steve regards the adoption of gearing as the beginning of the company's second stage of financing. The first stage she financed herself, by working for free; the second, 'growth', stage was financed by the willingness of panel members to wait a while before they were paid for their work.

Perhaps the qualms she felt about the gearing principle were what made her so receptive to the ideas of John Stevens when he joined the company as its first project manager in 1965. Stevens was a Liberal and a fervent advocate of the extension of share ownership. His arguments persuaded Steve Shirley and inspired her to embark on a tortuous and prolonged dialogue with the Inland Revenue aimed at transferring the equity of the company into the hands of the staff. By this time, in the mid-1960s, the panel numbered about sixty part-timers. A profit-sharing scheme was set up in 1966; it was this which would be replaced much later by the F International Trust.

One of the secrets of F International's success has been the balance that Steve Shirley has managed to maintain between a tightly knit headquarters team and a steadily growing panel of freelancers operating from home. She has pioneered new techniques for the management and control of outworkers which may well prove to be a pattern on which other companies, like Rank Xerox, will model their own schemes. There does not appear to have been much of a plan behind it apart from a wish to keep fixed costs as low as possible; it just worked out that way.

Now there are about 750 panel members of whom, on average, three-quarters are working at any one time. Back in 1966 the panel was less than a tenth of its present size, and the average 'utilisation' rate was considerably lower. The business mix in those days was varied, ranging from odd jobs to quite large projects. Steve likes large, fixed-price contracts because they allow forward planning, but she was always very aware of the risks associated with them.

Nowadays, the rule is that the company will not take on a project which accounts for more than 20 per cent of the total workload. In the early years the limit was more like 25 per cent. Perhaps 'limit' is the wrong word. It did not work quite like that. The trick, when a project that appeared to exceed the limit came along, was not to turn it down but to make sure that the rest of the business was built up sufficiently to keep the exposure to the big contract within reasonable bounds.

One example of a large job was a £40,000 contract, with progress payment clauses, for GEC. The work was part of the Concorde project and was to do specifically with the aircraft's 'black box' flight recorder. FPL's task was to design systems to manage the information being fed into the recorder. The trouble was that GEC, by now under the deft control of Arnold Weinstock, was a notoriously slow payer.

It got to the point when GEC owed £20,000 and when Steve Shirley had run out of patience. She went round to GEC's headquarters, determined to have it out with Weinstock. She failed to reach the great man himself, but she did manage to get a message through via a senior executive. A reply came back from Weinstock later that day: 'Tell Mrs Shirley that £20,000 is a significant sum for any business and that if she cares to come round tomorrow morning there will be a cheque waiting for her.' There was.

FPL and F International, as it became later, have had little trouble with bad debts. The clients are mostly blue chip and in any case it is Steve's experience that if you go round and sit determinedly in a late-payer's office, you rarely go away empty handed.

There have been other problem contracts though.

Quite early on, FPL won a substantial job of work, through Urwick Diebold again, from Castrol, part of the Burmah Oil group. Steve assigned one of her most talented panel members to the project. It went badly wrong. After six weeks, very little appeared to have been achieved. Steve became worried. If a large contract like that was to blow up in FPL's face it would do the young company's reputation no good at all. So she donned her 'troubleshooter' hat, left her husband looking after the baby, and went and sat in on the contract, working between 16 and 20 hours a day. She had to learn Fortran, a high-level computer language (it was for this task that she first called on John Stevens). In one week and two weekends she got the job working.

The company still discusses at some length so-called 'projects of concern', though these remain rare. It is not just if a customer is dissatisfied. Loss-making contracts are also given the detailed 'post mortem' treatment. An example was a job for the Sheffield Regional Hospital Board. It was worth £16,000 but the direct costs alone were over £24,000. The customer was quite happy, but the profit and loss account did not like it at all.

The financial record of F International to date can be divided roughly into two parts: the period up until the early 1970s during which the company was building up a clientele and was struggling, at times quite desperately, to keep its head above water, and the period since then which has seen a steady and, in recent years, an accelerating growth in both turnover and profits. In many ways the strength and resilience the company has demonstrated from about 1975 onwards is attributable to the tempering effect of an extremely difficult few years as the hopeful, outward-looking 1960s gave way to the grimmer, more introspective 1970s.

It was not that there had been no serious problems before. The cash-flow crisis which the generosity of Kit Grindley helped to extricate the company from was real enough.

And there was another time when Steve needed £1,600 so badly that she felt compelled to take out a second mortgage on their home. That was a husband-and-wife decision and a risky one. It was clear by then that their son was very badly handicapped. The prospect of having to move back with him into furnished digs cannot have been appealing.

But things were newer then – more experimental in a way. The lines along which the Shirleys' life together might have developed had FPL never existed were still more or less within reach. Less time and effort had been invested in the company at that stage. There was simply less to lose.

For entrepreneurs the crisis that hits their company in early maturity is usually the most traumatic. It tends to catch them off their guard. They are, by nature, optimists; there is no such person as a successful pessimist. When the initial act of entrepreneurial creation has been consolidated, when the company is up, running and clearly capable of further growth, when all systems seem to be go, the realisation that the whole thing could collapse overnight can come as a severe shock. Three things can happen on such occasions. The company can go bust and be heard of no more; it can survive in a state of suspended animation, staying still because it is too frightened to move; or it can, like F International, emerge considerably toughened by the experience.

The crisis in the early maturity of Steve Shirley's company was part financial and part personal. During the second half of the 1960s, when Steve was running a growing company more or less single-handedly from her home, she began to search for someone to share the burden with; someone who was not her husband or a friend or contact in the market her company was serving. She looked for her partner amongst the people she was interviewing for panel membership.

When she met Pamela Woodman she knew immediately she had found just the person. Pamela had complementary skills and the commercial acumen and apparently the commitment to share the load. Steve invited her to take shares in the company and become a true partner. Pamela declined. She wanted a salary and so that was how it was arranged. The two women established what they called a 'dual management system' and it worked very well for a time. And then the recession hit. The computerisation of British industry slowed down from a gallop to a trot and with the deceleration F International's market shrank. The inflow of work, which had been healthy and growing, reduced to a trickle. The company did its first ever mail shot.

Times were bad everywhere. Hardly a month would go by without news of the liquidation of a former client company. Steve realised she had not been quite as clever as she thought, that it had been partly the market that had taken FPL up in its early years and that it was not terribly well equipped for the down-phase of the business cycle.

And then, as if the recession was not enough, another and in many ways more painful blow came from an unexpected quarter. Pamela Woodman, her comrade-in-arms, her partner in all but equity, left the company, taking panel members and a chunk of precious business with her. Steve Shirley says the experience scarred her for life; 'that's where I got the toughness from. I found out what it was like in the hard times. I realised how much I cared.' She felt there was more at stake than the survival or otherwise of F International; a completely new way of organising work, which brought succour to the imprisoned mother and at the same time tapped a rich and under-exploited reserve of national talent, was in danger of being discredited. That she cared to good effect is shown by the fact that, after recording a loss of £3,815 in the year to 30 April 1972, the company recovered to register net profits of just under £2,000 in the following twelve months on substantially reduced turnover.

The idea of a breakaway group is a perennial nightmare for companies working in high-technology areas where exceptional skill and talent are at a premium. It happened once again, in Denmark, quite soon after the Scandinavian subsidiary was established in Copenhagen. It is surprising in a way that breakaways have not occurred more often. Entry costs into this market are low and since panel members are not contractually or logistically bound in any way to the headquarters operation, it would appear to be quite easy to get a reasonable size group together and lead it away. Many panel members work for other companies and there are also several who, for tax reasons mostly, have set up limited companies of their own.

But by and large the quality of management, the effectiveness of the control systems employed and perhaps still the charismatic influence of Steve Shirley, though she plays a much less visible role than she used to, have helped to keep F International and its panel members together. There may come a time when the size of the company passes a critical point, but there is no sign of it yet. Steve emphasises that home-grown managers like Suzette Harold, Mary Smith, Penny Tutt, Alison Newell and Janet Lennon amongst many others have helped enormously to maintain the cohesion of the group.

When Steve Shirley decided to reorganise the corporate structure of FPL and to group it under a holding company, there was little justification for the 'International' in the new name. There had been the odd overseas contract, the first for a company in Antwerp which was the occasion of a rather clumsy attempt to get to grips with foreign language documentation. The customer was very happy with the work but found F International's French pretty hard going.

The first serious attempt to make good the International name began in the early 1970s with the help of the company's then chairman Frank Knight who had worked in Europe before, though not in the computing services field. He and Steve began to look at Europe in earnest with a view to establishing an overseas operation. They had in mind not merely the computing services product but also the *modus operandi* of F International enunciated in the company's stated employment policy: 'To utilise, wherever practicable, the services of people who are unable to work in a conventional office-based environment.'

Denmark was chosen for a number of reasons: Frank Knight had good contacts there, English is widely spoken and the English are well-liked. In addition, Denmark was regarded as a convenient gateway into the large Scandinavian market. But Denmark's greatest attraction was the relatively high proportion of women in the data-processing industry – in so far as the F International method was concerned, that seemed to make Denmark the obvious choice.

Looking back now, Steve Shirley admits that 'our evaluation of the social situation in Denmark was not very clever.' What she and Frank Knight had failed to spot was that the main reason for the high proportion of women in the Danish data processing industry was the fact that Denmark had evolved over the years a much more sophisticated child-care system than had Britain. The practical problems of mixing motherhood with work are less in Denmark, though of course the emotional and psychological difficulties are just as great as here.

But the Danish venture went ahead anyway, based on the idea of referring work obtained there back to the UK. For several years precious little happened, and looking back now it is clear that the venture was seriously under-capitalised. Eventually it was decided to hire the services of local systems analysts, working on a freelance basis, to carry out feasibility studies and then to refer the bulk programming work back home. The scheme worked; the branch was incorporated into the first overseas subsidiary, F International ApS, and the search began for a second continental outpost.

They missed out the branch stage this time and went straight for a subsidiary company based in The Hague. The Dutch economy was booming at the time, the F International formula went down well and the business began coming in nicely.

Then things began to go badly wrong in Denmark. The operation, based from the outset on the idea of a largely autonomous venture led by an entrepreneurially-minded local manager, proved increasingly difficult to control and administer. Eventually, after seven years, the local manager started a parallel operation and had to be dismissed. F International had to start all over again. Denmark 2 was better organised, but once again Steve Shirley yielded to the temptation of leaving things to the new Danish manager who then left, again without a proper handover. This time the lessons were learned properly; Denmark 3 is in profit now and is the object of regular monthly control from Britain.

Similar problems arose in Holland. The agent left without a proper handover and the subsidiary had to be re-launched, properly capitalised and adequately controlled from home. There were other problems too. The Hague might have seemed to be the most international city, being the seat of government and the capital, but it quickly became obvious that Amsterdam was the only place to be. F International BV is now based in Amsterdam, on the Herengracht. Another problem peculiar to Holland was the employment protection laws. They made it very difficult to apply the F International methods. Dutch employment legislation virtually disavows the very idea of freelance workers and has required much tinkering with short-term contracts and notice periods.

The basic demand is there all right in most countries, but cultural and legislative differences can make it hard to winkle out a formula for implementing F International's unique employment policies. They are exportable, but not in their pure, original form. One wonders whether an equivalent of F International would ever have emerged had Steve Shirley grown up in Holland or Denmark. It may be that the peculiarities of the British social system were themselves essential for the development of the company.

F International's experiences in Europe have taught the company the importance of maintaining tight control over the staff management functions in overseas subsidiaries and have highlighted the risks associated with relying too much on the entrepreneurial abilities of local agents.

The lessons learned from America are rather different. Through a chance meeting at a conference in Barcelona in 1978, F International decided to enter into a relationship with a new company called Heights Information Technology Systems. In contrast to the European ventures, the strategy here was not to go out and win business but to license the F International employment system; to export the way in which the services were supplied rather than the services themselves.

As Steve Shirley put it in a speech she gave to the European Computer Services Association in Copenhagen in June 1982: 'We arranged a licence agreement whereby, for what at the time seemed a sensible sum of money, F International would license Heights to use our work methods, copy and Americanise all our working proformas, control techniques, and we would help them recruit from scratch, train and develop a small, newly financed company.'

The contract proved a loss-maker and was not renewed when it expired after two years. F International felt it needed more money for its services while Heights felt it could not afford to pay more. But even so Steve regarded the venture as a success. F International's methods have been introduced successfully at two Heights branches in New York and California and, despite the decision not to renew the contract, the relationship between the two companies remained close. Ultimately, early in 1983, F International acquired the company and thus for the first time had a wholly-owned subsidiary in the huge US market.

And there has been functional as well as geographical expansion. The company has launched a computer training division on the back of its own in-house training systems and is keen to build up its computer consultancy activities through the panel as well as through head office.

The regionalisation of the business in the UK market, made possible by the delegation of project management responsibilities to panel members, gives the company a good national spread, though it is recognised that it has probably increased the risk of further breakaways.

A more radical departure is the establishment of an associate company, Systematix, to exploit the booming microcomputer business systems market. The company has been founded on the basis of new software methods for systems generation pioneered by Steve Shirley's long-time friend and ally Kit Grindley, currently working for Systematix. Technically the company reckons to be two years ahead of its nearest rival. In Steve's view the main task is to crack the marketing problem and be in a position to sell to small businesses rather than to the *Times* top 1,000.

F International recently paid £300,000 for its new headquarters in Berkhamsted which financial controller Donald Stewart says 'has put some guts into the balance sheet'.

Systematix takes up some space there at the moment but will probably move out once it gets firmly established. It is a tribute to the effectiveness of the F International method that quite ambitious expansion and diversification plans can be drawn up in the knowledge that the elegant but modestly proportioned headquarters will remain adequate for the foreseeable future.

Meantime, Steve Shirley herself has been seduced into becoming a more public figure. Her advice is regularly sought by institutions both public and private and her energy and commitment to things that interest her are much in demand. Between 1979 and 1982 she was an active Vice-President of the British Computer Society (BCS), helping to re-structure the organisation so that it reflects more accurately the changes that are going on in the industry. She has helped to guide the BCS towards seeking chartered status. She was the inspiration behind the BCS 'Young Computing Funfair' which she mounted in 1979 and she also organised an exhibition of micro-based aids for disabled people in the House of Commons in July 1981.

During the International Year for Disabled People she was involved in a number of projects linking Information Technology to the needs of the disabled and she chaired the BCS Review team which reported on the confidentiality arrangements for the 1981 Census. She is a member of the Department of Industry's Electronics and Avionics Requirements Board and the chairman of its Computing and Communications Committee. She was a member of the ACARD Working Party on Information Technology which reported to the Cabinet Office in 1980 and she is a busy consulting editor on information processing for the John Wiley & Sons publishing house. In 1980 she was awarded the OBE for services to the computing industry.

Her entry into public life was tentative at first. She became interested in involving herself with the wider industry of which her company is a part when she felt that F International no longer needed her. She gave up the chairmanship for a while in 1973, but took up what she calls 'front-lining' again in 1978. The second time round she threw herself into extra-curricular activities with more relish. Her OBE gave her confidence and she now enjoys government work immensely.

It appears at the moment that her greatest interest is the development of British excellence in the field of Artificial Intelligence. She was one of thirty industrialists invited by the Department of Industry to discuss the Japanese 'Fifth Generation Project' early in 1982 and she was interested in establishing a

Knowledge Engineering 'goal' for the British computing industry.

Unlike the other profiles in this book, the story of F International and Steve Shirley is one of managerial and organisational rather than scientific and technological innovation. Steve spotted an opportunity in the labour market and in her endeavours to exploit it she developed a working method which is unique and at the same time pregnant with possibilities.

The story illustrates one of the classic entrepreneurial qualities: a refusal to take things for granted. In the early 1960s, when Freelance Programmers was formed, it was generally assumed that when a woman wanted to have a child and wanted to be with her children while they grew up, she was obliged to withdraw from the labour market. It was the way things were in those days and it looked as if it was the way things would remain. Working women who wish to become mothers face a cruel choice – either give up work at what will often be a crucial stage in their career or stay on and pay someone else to enjoy the pleasure of raising their children.

The story of F International is, to a large extent, the story of one woman's rejection of that choice.

The existence and prosperity of a company like F International is also corroboration of a kind for my main thesis – that rapid technological change has consequences that extend far beyond the technology itself. The pace of change represents a major upheaval in the system of production and puts a high premium on flexibility.

F International is an extremely flexible organisation. It can exist profitably under a very wide range of market conditions because its structure imparts to the company powerful self-stabilising qualities. In more technical terms one might say that the company's fixed costs are an unusually small proportion of its total costs. It is hard to say whether it was inevitable that a company with such a structure would move towards a co-operative kind of organisation, or whether the F International Trust is entirely the result of Steve Shirley's own personality and predispositions.

The most notably successful co-operatives in Britian this century have been the creatures, for the most part, of idealistic entrepreneurs. John Spedan Lewis set up the John Lewis Partnership by giving away shares in the company to his employees; Francis Impey and Oliver Morland did the same at office equipment group Kalamazoo; it was the charismatic personality of Ernest Bader which formed Scott Bader.

As we have seen, it was the principle of 'gearing' which first started Steve Shirley thinking about co-operative structures – that, and the catalytic influence of John Stevens.

Stevens felt that workers should be given shares rather than be required to buy them. At first Steve Shirley felt equity should be earned; the company's first individual shareholders were those who worked for free or for next to nothing at various critical times. By about 1968 Steve had begun to employ consultants to help work out some kind of share/profit participation scheme. They supported her original view, that equity should be reserved for those who made the most important contributions to the business. But by then Steve's ideas had progressed. She now believed equity participation should be a matter of right rather than of reward. The profit-sharing scheme, which was always intended to be an interim measure, went right down to the office cleaner. It was phased out because of cash shortages and the demotivating effect of a long run of nil bonuses.

By 1975, following the expenditure of much time and money, Steve was ready to present a paper to the board. She describes what happened: 'All was spoilt because I used the emotive word "co-operative" when we had a Chief Executive, Suzette Harold, who is a devout Conservative. "If you do, I'll go", she said. So that was that!'

But gradually the doubters were won round to the idea of a trust and there followed a three-year legal haul to get the paperwork cleared. The problem was that the relevant legislation only applied to employee trusts and only 10 per cent of F International's workforce is employed, the rest being panel members. This has required that for the time being at least, the trust is couched in terms of employees only, though the trustees are also mindful of responsibilities to the freelancers. The aim is to get 49 per cent of the company into the trust before Steve Shirley retires and for her to bequeath the rest. No tax is payable if *all* her shares go in on her death.

The early purchases are made according to a formula along

the lines of the Kalamazoo system where the Kalamazoo Workers' Alliance gradually accumulated a controlling stake in the company with the proceeds of a profit-sharing scheme. Steve Shirley acknowledges her debt to the examples of the John Lewis Partnership, Kalamazoo and another profitable co-operative, Geographers A-Z. It is too early to say whether the co-operative will become a common corporate form as business adapts to the new conditions, but it does seem likely that equity will be more widely spread within companies than it has been.

Finally, it is worth noting that the existence of co-operatives like the F International Trust, the Scott Bader Commonwealth and the John Lewis Partnership casts doubt on the widespread belief that entrepreneurs are motivated mainly by the desire for wealth. Steve Shirley is the opposite of acquisitive. She has a mink coat which she regards as a bit of a joke and as costume for 'role-playing' and she drives a BL Mini of the 1275 GT variety.

So if it was not money that motivated her, what was it . . . a determination to prove a point, a desire to liberate a few hundred women from some of the constraints of motherhood, a wish to be in control of her own destiny, a fascination with the science of computing or perhaps it was the simple pleasure she took in playing the business game with skill in a world run by men?

5

Mike Bevan and Xionics

Though it would be premature to predict that a small British company, employing a few dozen people, will soon begin to obscure the lustre of the mighty IBM, there is no doubt that rapid technological change does offer giantkilling possibilities. The story of Mike Bevan and Xionics shows that there are chinks in the armour of the seemingly most impregnable of large companies – chinks that can sometimes be probed and enlarged.

Michael Bevan was born on the day Hitler invaded Czechoslovakia and was christened on the day Britain declared war on Germany. He grew up in Gloucestershire, the second eldest of three gifted brothers. He won the prize for Spanish at the Crypt Grammar School in Gloucester and obtained grade 1 'O' levels in French and Spanish. In his mid-teens he looked on course for a place at university, reading modern languages.

But times were hard in those days in the second half of the 1950s, family money was short and National Service was looming. Mike left school and went to work as a clerk at a branch of the Midland Bank in Gloucester. When the call to arms came in 1958 he chose to spend his two years in the Royal Air Force. He began to prepare for university entrance while serving. He took 'A' levels in French, Spanish and English and in his spare time he started a cricket team at the base. When the time came, Bevan started the rounds of the universities in search of a place. He went to a number of interviews, thought about it, and decided to give varsity a miss. He had been dismayed by how young everyone seemed at university and during National Service he had been working with people who were earning twice as much as the £217 a year he had been paid as a bank clerk. He felt that another three years of studying before he would be financially independent was just too long.

Given Mike Bevan's background and given the sort of people in his peer group, the decision not to go to university must rank as a significant one. If he had his time again, it is not at all clear that he would make the same choice. But he believes that not having gone was an advantage in some ways. There is a certain rebelliousness about his thinking which might have been smoothed out and more important, if he had gone to university, he would probably not have ended up in the computer industry.

In 1961 Mike Bevan joined the headquarters establishment of the Ministry of Works at Lambeth, in London, as an Executive Officer. In his first week he received a circular letter inviting him to apply for entry into the new Automatic Data Processing (ADP) section. The Ministry was shortly to take delivery of an ICT 1301 computer. Mike applied, passed the tests and was accepted. He got on well with the people and was fascinated by the technology. 'I was sent on a programming course,' he recalls, 'and then I got stuck in. I found that it was what I had been looking for all my life.'

Bevan was fortunate in having as a boss a man called Harry Ayre, one of the true trail-blazers on the user side of the industry. Mike says of Ayre, 'He is one of the two or three most gifted people I have ever met.' Ayre's interests included the 'portability' of software – the degree to which computer programs could be run on different types of machine. He has the distinction of having written a complete Cobol compiler, single-handed, in six months. It is normally reckoned to take three or four man-years to write a compiler.

Mike himself was working on adapting compilers (programs that translate statements of the users' requirements into the binary language a computer uses), memory-sorting routines and system software. He was already interested by now in the ways and means of linking computers up with other bits of equipment. He began to develop a reputation as a 'device handler' ace.

Bevan remembers it as being very exciting. There was no clock-watching; often programmers could be found still hard at work at 2 or 3 o'clock in the morning. There was a sense of urgency, of the need to press on and an Ayre-inspired emphasis on getting things right first time. Bevan says, 'Working with Harry meant that I grew up assuming that programming errors were the exception rather than the rule.'

Computer skills were in short supply in the early 1960s and it was not long before Mike Bevan's special qualities became apparent outside the Ministry. He was approached in 1964 by ICT (later to become ICL) and he agreed to join the company's Stevenage laboratories as a principal engineer. His main job was to develop programs for testing the capabilities of the company's new 1900 series of computers.

Two years later, in June 1966, Bevan was approached by two Midlands businessmen. They had heard of a new phenomenon called a 'software house' and they wanted to invest in one. The idea was that they would be sleeping partners in a company run by Bevan. Mike would have a controlling share and they would provide 'drip-feed' finance as and when it was required. Bevan agreed and the M. J. Bevan Limited software house was born. There was trouble almost immediately.

The Labour government under Harold Wilson, elected two years previously, introduced the Selective Employment Tax (SET), designed as an instrument of industrial re-structuring in what Wilson described as 'the white heat of technological change'. Opinions still differ about the effectiveness or otherwise of the SET, but one thing is for sure – the tax selected against the Midlands engineering company which was the source of M. J. Bevan Ltd's development finance.

The money dried up and Bevan was left on his own, trying to sell software services to companies which could not afford or could not find their own programmers. He was fortunate in that his wife Mary, whom he had married in 1964, was still working at the Ministry of Works where the couple had met. Mike says, 'that was one of the things that made it possible'. The first contract came from the Lea Valley Water Company and was worth about £600. Marketing in those early days was a question of reading the papers, spotting who was advertising for DP staff and then ringing them up and saying 'You don't know me, but . . .'

The first big break came six months later when someone Bevan had known at ICT left to join English Electric (soon to become part of ICT). The man remembered Bevan's special skills and when problems were encountered with test software for EE's System Four computer, M. J. Bevan Limited was awarded a large contract. Though Mike did not get closely involved with System Four itself, he developed an intimate relationship with a purpose-built tool for testing the main computer's peripheral equipment. The machine was known as the System Four Device Tester (SFDT).

When it was first introduced, the only way to talk to the SFDT was to juggle with an array of binary switches on the front. Mike keyed in a small 'assembler' language so that the machine could read punched paper tape and later he added a disc drive and an operating system.

Standing back and surveying his handiwork Bevan concluded that the SFDT was now a competent and versatile device in its own right, and might be highly marketable (the word 'mini-computer' was not yet fashionable). He suggested as much to the English Electric people he was working with. They did not see it. When they looked at the SFDT they saw a tool, not a product.

Meantime M. J. Bevan Ltd was prospering, as were many of the other software houses. In 1969, when Bevan made his sadly ignored suggestion about the SFDT, the company was employing 180 people and was doing business in Sweden, Hungary, Poland, Bulgaria and Czechoslovakia. The firm had a marketing director and a management structure.

The success of the independent software houses during the 1960s had a great deal to do with the generation gap. The computer industry was still new, and though the senior executives of large companies came to appreciate the importance of the technology, they always found it hard to come to terms with the fact that the 'experts' were invariably young, long-haired and difficult to manage. It was thus a great convenience for them to be able to 'farm out' data-processing work to independent companies, run by men and women who were themselves young enough, and sufficiently enthusiastic about the technology, to get the best out of that unbiddable breed of programmers. This technological aspect of the generation gap was as evident in the public as it was in the private sector. Mike Bevan, thanks partly to his stint at the Ministry of Works, won a great deal of business for his company from government.

He also won the hidden part of the most controversial software contract of the day, for the London Airport Cargo Expedition System (LACES). The LACES contract was worth about £50,000 and most of the independent software houses went for it. It was awarded to the world's largest software house, Computer Sciences Corporation of the US. The technical press expressed dismay at the decision not to 'buy British' and the LACES contract became something of an industry *cause célèbre*.

The hardware contract went to English Electric and this was where M. J. Bevan Ltd got in on the act. They won a contract from EE to develop a special software system which EE needed for the development of the LACES hardware.

But there were cash-flow problems associated with working for large companies. At one time Bevan was doing about £10,000 worth of business a month with GEC and sometimes he had to wait six months for payment. Mike still rates as one of his greatest business coups his success in persuading GEC to issue him with bills of exchange at the start of large contracts. These were promises to pay M. J. Bevan Ltd such and such a sum on such and such a date. They were negotiable, which means they could be sold to a bank or to some other financial institution for a large fraction of their nominal value.

Another good wheeze was the exploitation of a rule being applied in government at the time which required contract negotiators to take early payment discounts if they were offered. Thenceforth Bevan quoted two prices when bidding for government work – the nominal and the 'discount' price which was 5 per cent lower and was available if payment was received within seven days.

The company was doing well by the turn of the decade. It had moved out of Mike Bevan's home in 1967 into a three-room suite above a jeweller's shop in Hitchin and other premises were found later nearby. There was also an office in Manchester to serve English Electric and Marconi.

An indication of the company's standing in the industry was that when the Software Houses Association was established, Mike Bevan was collared on the pavement outside the Cafe Royal where the inaugural meeting was to be held and persuaded to stand for the chairmanship of the new body. His supporters were anxious to prevent it from being dominated by the big boys like CAP, run by Alex D'Agapeyeff and Tony Hardcastle. Bevan was elected chairman of the SHA and Hardcastle became deputy chairman.

When I first met Mike Bevan in the summer of 1982, he was riding high on the back of an idea that he expected and still expects to make a pretty big splash in what is known as 'networking' technology. His company was at an early stage of its development, but it had already made contact with the venture-capital industry. Bevan had for some years been highly sceptical of the British venture capitalists, for one reason or another, and said of them that, as far as he could see, 'they wanted to take the venture and the capital out of venture capital.'

Bevan admitted then, in mid-1982, that things appeared to be changing for the better, but his view of British venture capital in the 1970s is by no means an unusual one. There was and remains a widespread feeling that during the 1970s our financial institutions were negligent. They are charged with having done their country a great disservice by failing to provide a proper lubricant for the technological explosion that had just begun.

One of the reasons for this lapidary posture, particularly in so far as it involved the big pension funds, may have been the fate of a bold investment experiment launched in 1967. In financial circles and particularly in the opinionated world of financial journalism, the public circumstances of this experiment's failure gave to the company concerned, Spey Investments, something of the reputation of a *folie de grandeur*.

It was the brainchild of an able and charismatic businessman called Charles Gordon. Spey was, in many ways, the forerunner of the modern venture-capital company, containing several of the elements that are nowadays recognised, on the other side of the Atlantic at least, to be of fundamental importance in venture-capital investment. Gordon persuaded a number of institutions to pool a large amount of money and to make it available to Spey for venture-capital investment. The idea was that a team of first-rate managers would go out into the highways and byways of the corporate undergrowth, looking for tightly-run, high-technology companies in need of expansion finance and management support.

In 1970 the eyes of Spey's company hunters fell on M. J. Bevan Ltd.

Bevan remembers vividly his one and only meeting with Charles Gordon in Spey's sumptuous offices at 10 Old Jewry in the City of London, where he was 'knee deep in carpet'. But he found the man impressive, even so. Though Gordon knew little about the technical side of the computer industry, he went, in Bevan's view, straight to the heart of the software industry's commercial predicament. He suggested that a software company's profit opportunities were fundamentally limited by the fact that it could only take on more business if it could recruit more programmers.

Bevan agreed with the analysis but said there was an answer. He told Gordon about the software 'package' – the closest the industry has so far got to the mass-produced product. Bevan explained that if a software company could identify a relatively large market for a particular kind of software system, and could go away and write a *general* answer to the problems the system was designed to solve, then it could sell the 'package' several times over.

Gordon liked the idea. It was agreed that Spey would buy out Bevan's original backers and would supply the company with cash to develop a 'packaged software' product line. It was understood, though never stated explicitly, that Spey's 'exit route' would be by public flotation on the stock market of M. J. Bevan Ltd at some future date.

The relationship worked well to begin with. Spey's policy was to use its team of top-rank business talent actively – to adopt, as the modern parlance has it, a 'hands-on' investment policy. This was not then and never needs to be the same as an 'interfering' investment policy. Bevan recruited a team and began work on the first of the new products. It was a vehicle-scheduling package called TRANSIT for any company anxious to use its vehicle fleet more efficiently. TRANSIT was ahead of its time and is still in use.

But at the end of 1970, when TRANSIT was nearing completion, Mike Bevan's metabolism went on strike. Eighteen hours a day was too much; he contracted double pneumonia, swiftly followed by double pleurisy. He was out of action for two months and when he returned to work he found he had lost much of his drive and enthusiasm. Everything suddenly looked too big and non-technical. The market was weakening fast by then. Customers were going bust and major contracts were being cancelled or deferred. Bevan set about the painful task of cutting staff – 'reducing the head count' as he called it. It was not reduced fast enough and the company began to record losses.

Spey was providing limited additional funds to help out, but Charles Gordon's dream was also beginning to turn sour. His institutional backers pulled out one by one and the financial press began baying for blood. Eventually another company, the Synergy Group, agreed to provide funds for M. J. Bevan Ltd which was by then back in the black and convalescing well. As a result of the deal, Bevan lost control. The press laid the blame wholly on Spey, but Bevan himself thinks that was unfair. He says, 'I was terribly naive. I didn't know enough about running companies or about financial institutions.'

Mike decided it was time for a rest. He went into self-imposed retirement which only ended at the end of 1972 when Tony Hardcastle of CAP suggested Bevan join him in the formation of a new company called Triad Computing Systems. Triad was financed by the British Oxygen Company which held a 40 per cent equity stake. Hardcastle and colleagues had the rest of the shares, some of which were set aside for Bevan, if and when he should want them.

After his experiences with his own company, Mike was not particularly enamoured of the idea of a prolonged association with another new firm so he said he would work at Triad for a couple of years and would then see how he felt about staying on. He was well known in the industry by then and was never short of job offers. However, the Triad deal was an opportunity to pursue his entrepreneurial instincts in partnership with a man who was widely regarded as one of the most competent financial managers in the computer services industry.

The idea was that Hardcastle should go after the big, mainframe contracts he had been dealing with at CAP, such as the long and lucrative project CAP had with Phoenix Assurance in Bristol, while Bevan would concentrate on supplying technical software for mini-computers.

Most significantly, in the light of the direction in which Bevan's technical interests were moving, he negotiated marketing rights for a package developed by the National Physical Laboratory, called SCRAPBOOK. It was the first ever commercially available office automation system. It was screen-based and offered text, filing and retrieval facilities. The Ministry of Defence liked SCRAPBOOK but would have liked it even more if it could have been run on hardware made by a certain large UK company (let's call it company 'X'). So Mike Bevan went to company 'X' and said that all they had to do was spend about £10,000 on a software job for their existing computer system and the SCRAPBOOK hardware contract was theirs. Company 'X' seemed very interested and a number of meetings followed. A proposal was put to the board with every confidence that it would be accepted. The board turned it down. Triad's SCRAPBOOK deal with the MoD went ahead, but without company 'X' hardware.

Another Bevan/Triad contract (Mike was effectively being 'body-shopped' at the time) was for Plessey. The group had identified, through its long-range planning committee, the looming importance of business communications. Bevan was asked to investigate the possibilities for linking word-processing, text, paging and other business activities to Plessey's mainstream telecommunications products.

Plessey's interest in business communications at this time, an interest that was to grow in the years ahead, is a fine example of the phenomenon known in the electronics industry as 'convergence'. Data processing (computers) and data communications (telephones and the like) were beginning in the mid-1970s to move towards each other.

It was becoming clear that the two technologies were destined to meet in business communications systems, which were going to comprise a very large market indeed.

Telecommunications companies like Plessey were thus acquiring data-processing technology and skills while preparing their attack on the market through telephone exchanges, while at the same time computer companies were acquiring an understanding of data communications while preparing their attack on the same market through computers. It remains to be seen which approach will prove the most successful; the major confrontation is likely to be between the two US giants, IBM and AT&T.

'Convergence' was also the background to another Bevan contract, this time with ITT. The American company had a telephone exchange which appeared to the group's long-range planners to offer a way in to business systems. Bevan was asked to take a close look at the exchange and to investigate its potential for handling data as well as voice. Further ITT business followed.

Another important contract was a job Bevan took on for Midland Bank's then recently acquired travel agency company, Thomas Cook. Midland had backed a small computer systems company, let's call it Anteater Computer Systems (ACS), run by a flamboyant American. The attraction for the bank was a specialised computer terminal that ACS was developing for foreign exchange dealing. The development went wrong and the company ran into financial difficulties. Two years earlier Bevan had made something of a name for himself by helping to sort out what remained after the collapse of Business Computers Limited and he was asked by Thomas Cook to do a similar job on ACS. As with BCL, it was a question of salvaging those bits of the company that were technically advanced and might therefore have commercial value.

It was just after the Court Line crash and soon after Midland's acquisition of Thomas Cook. ACS was relatively small beer, but Midland was none the less anxious not to be associated with a messy failure that might attract adverse publicity. Bevan closed down all ACS premises, apart from the factory, and all but 20 of the staff were dismissed. The job was begun under a 'body-shopping' contract with Triad, but after six months Bevan was offered the chairmanship of ACS and was asked to follow the terminal project through. He agreed to stay for a further six months, during which he completed the development and delivered 120 systems to Thomas Cook, including 350 special-purpose terminals for foreign exchange dealing. These systems are still in continuous daily use.

The technical feature of the ACS terminal that interested Bevan most was its use of a gadget known as a processor 'emulator'. While pondering the principles of the device, he suddenly thought that here was a low-cost way for established companies to exploit new markets. Armed with this idea, Mike went to the same company 'X' which had rejected his proposal about SCRAPBOOK.

At the time IBM was on the point of launching its business mini-computer on the UK market and there was no comparable home-grown competitor. Bevan suggested that company 'X' should hire ACS (by then re-named Comet Computing Services) to 'emulate' that same mainframe Bevan had wanted to get SCRAPBOOK to run on, so that a new, much cheaper version could be launched as an IBM-beating business mini. The idea was attractive to the technical and marketing people in the company 'X' computer division. They were under orders from above to increase their sales, and the addition of a runner in the booming mini market, without the need for a prolonged and costly development process, seemed an ideal way forward.

Bevan proposed that the standard software library already available on the mainframe should be supplemented by a range of 'packaged' commercial software to be developed by a software house. He had his eye on the emulation contract for Comet and he suggested to a friend of his who had just left Triad to join Data Logic (DL) that DL should go for the software business. DL liked the idea and so did the Department of Industry which offered financial support. Bevan was asked by company 'X' and DL to carry out the detailed investigation and planning, covering hardware and software development, documentation, sales planning and funding.

All seemed set when the whole project was quashed by a company 'X' board decision. Bevan does not know why exactly, but he suspects it was something to do with the notorious 'not invented here' syndrome. He believes the company 'X' directors reasoned that if a small engineering company could develop a new computer for company 'X', then the mighty company 'X' could surely do something similar itself. And sure enough, eighteen months later, company 'X' did indeed launch a mini-computer based on its larger machine. Bevan thinks they made a serious mistake, however, by supplying the mini only with custom-made software rather than with packages which Bevan had long been convinced were the secret of success in the mini market.

Acts of creation, it is said, come out of the blue but not out of a vacuum. The prepared mind is a pre-condition for the insight. Leading up to a night in late 1975, when Bevan, while worrying the idea of a computer business system on the edge of sleep, was suddenly overwhelmed by a great idea, there were several years of unconscious preparation.

During his attempts to sell SCRAPBOOK as a separate system he had encountered the problem of providing users with access to information already held on their company's mainframe machine. Later, during his work for the telecommunications groups ITT and Plessey, he had emphasised repeatedly to his clients that it was not sufficient to think of the technology of business systems solely from the point of view of computer suppliers. It seemed clear to Bevan that as more and more suppliers began to offer computers and office automation systems which were wholly incompatible with each other, these problems of communications and access were bound to increase alarmingly.

During Bevan's time at ACS he had investigated the possibility of producing a microprocessor-based 'personal' computer developed from the Heath Robinson devices that had just begun to appear in the US. Bevan reckoned that once cheap, powerful, desk-top machines like these began to appear in any quantity, access and communications problems would be cropping up everywhere. He became convinced that by the late 1970s and early 1980s, this growing problem of incompatibility would emerge as the most serious obstacle to the co-ordinated development of business information systems.

The first step towards his solution was the recognition that all computers – mainframes, minis, word-processors, personal computers – engage in two types of activity: the *processing* of information and the *management* of information.

Information management covers everything to do with storing, retrieving, organising, protecting and communicating data. All computers need it and yet most computers employ completely different management methods.

The reason for this is that it has not, so far, been in the

interests of the major hardware suppliers to adopt common standards. They prefer to sell their names rather than individual products and this has led them to try to protect their existing customer bases by making all their machines as different from those of their rivals as possible. This approach, which has nothing to do with technology and everything to do with marketing, has resulted in the prevalence of what is known as the 'closed architecture' system.

Employing Mike Bevan's own analogy, imagine what would have happened had there been, from the outset, a comparable lack of standards for telephone systems. 'We would', he suggests, 'have seen mainframe, mini and micro telephone exchanges, each with its own dialling method, signal characteristics, telephone numbering systems, etc. Inter-exchange communication would have required the development of countless special connection boxes.'

Having identified the lack of information management standards as the lock on the door to more 'open' architectures, Mike Bevan went in search of a key. Referring again to his telephone exchange analogy, he asked himself what would happen if there existed an equivalent device that might be called a 'data exchange'. This would handle all data-management operations at a particular site, providing processing systems with a simple, standard connection through which they could get their data.

With such an arrangement a personal computer could use the same data as an IBM or ICL mainframe. Inter-system connections would be completely automatic and the data exchange itself would be the perfect vehicle for introducing data management and communications standards if and when they were finally agreed. Once the idea was there, the hardware more or less designed itself.

It would have to contain large numbers of storage devices, each equipped with a processor to control it and provide access to the attached computers; it would need a network to distribute the data around the building; it would need a number of conversion boxes and software packages to enable computers of different types to be connected and provision would have to be made for temporary access, pending full incorporation of existing data bases locked up in mainframe machines.

This was the philosopher's stone of network engineering

which would break open systems architecture once and for all and in so doing would change decisively the direction of technological development.

For obvious reasons, associated with the closed architecture tradition referred to above, none of the large companies was likely to be interested in such a product; on the contrary, they would be inclined to squash hurriedly any suggestion of this kind if a member of their research and development teams had the temerity to suggest anything so scandalous. So Mike Bevan's musings on such matters in mid-1975, culminating in a flash of inspiration while he was lying in bed one night, were by no means idle. His entrepreneurial instincts had identified, perhaps unconsciously, a genuine market opportunity. It was not that there would be no demand for such a system, quite the reverse; it was that none of the established computer companies would be willing to supply it.

Bevan's flash of inspiration embodies what have come to be known as 'local area networks' and 'back end data base processors'. From these he designed a 'converged architecture' office system employing 'transparent data exchange'. He recognised the idea immediately as something that was powerful enough to build a whole new business on.

When Data Logic offered Bevan the sort of job he had grown accustomed to, a sort of roving consultancy commission, it was natural for him to put his new idea, which he had christened the DATABUS, to the three DL entrepreneurs, Alan Thomas, Alan Wood and Robin Davis. They agreed to retain Bevan's services to seek funding on DL's behalf for the DATABUS development. Having acquired a grant from the Department of Industry for a feasibility study, Bevan began to hawk the project around the large companies. There was interest but no commitment of funds.

The venture-capital organisations were also approached, but this was before the dawn of their enlightenment and the response was 'It sounds very interesting Mr. Bevan, but if it's as good as you say, why isn't IBM doing it?'

The National Research Development Corporation (NRDC) offered to fund half the estimated £300,000 research and development budget if DL would put up the rest. DL was only prepared to offer £30,000, leaving a £120,000 deficiency. Alan

Thomas proposed an alternative solution. He suggested that Bevan should shelve DATABUS for the time being and should instead launch a DL subsidiary called Micro Logic to offer customised electronic engineering services for the emergent microcomputer technology. The idea was that Micro Logic would 'pump-prime' the DATABUS project by earning enough money to fund the heavy R&D budget.

Micro Logic was conspicuously successful from the word go. Its first contract was for Grand Metropolitan, the hotels and brewing giant. GrandMet had a communications problem and wanted a 'black box' to solve it. Bevan and his Micro Logic team developed a device called a 'statistical multiplexer' which the customer bought in large numbers and still uses.

Another job was for Allied Breweries (now Allied-Lyons) which was having trouble with its stocktaking systems. The contract with Micro Logic was for the design and development of a portable microcomputer for stocktaking. Allied funded the work on a month-by-month basis, and once the device had been developed and tested its production was transferred to Systime Limited. Called 'Microframe', the portable computer met its target weight of 20 lb and included an integral printer. It was equivalent to, and pre-dated by some years, the modern Osborne portable microcomputer. Bevan believes DL could have made a great deal more money out of it had more adventurous pricing and marketing policies been adopted. Even so, the contract was handsomely profitable.

Then, just before Micro Logic's success became substantial enough to trigger the DATABUS agreement, DL's owners sold their company to the American computer and electronics group, Raytheon, for £3.3 million.

This was the signal for Bevan to depart. 'The last thing I wanted,' he says, 'was to develop DATABUS for a US company.'

Alan Thomas stayed with Raytheon, pocketing his £500,000 entrepreneurial reward, but after a decent interval Alan Wood and Robin Davis departed. With the proceeds of their DL shares they set up a venture-capital company called Multihavens and agreed to provide £40,000 of seed-corn funding for Xionics Limited, the company Bevan had just set up as the vehicle for DATABUS. Xionics was incorporated in late-1979. Its stated objective was 'the development and exploitation of a highly innovative "Office of the Future" integrated architecture for corporate information systems.'

I described Mike Bevan's fund-raising strategy on his second cap-in-hand tour, directed this time at users rather than suppliers, in a *Financial Weekly* article in July 1982:

> The scene is the headquarters of one of the giant multinational corporations. The phone rings in the office of the director in charge of communications.
>
> 'Hello . . . a new telecommunications product? What does it do? . . . sounds interesting. How much does it cost? . . . Phew!, that's a bit steep. When can you demonstrate it? . . . You haven't built it yet? . . . You want to be paid in advance?
>
> 'Let me get this straight. You have an idea for a new system and you want us to finance the building of a prototype by paying you 80 per cent of the purchase price in advance. Is that right?'

It was not, as I suggested in the article, a very orthodox way of going about the task of raising money. The approach indicates how passionately Bevan believed in DATABUS (now called XIBUS) and its success shows how evident the divergence of interest between computer suppliers and computer users had become by the late 1970s.

Bevan, who had been joined by Ian Richardson, one of Britain's leading computer systems and software designers, secured his advance development funding from BP Oil, the Calor Group, Scottish Gas, the Littlewoods Organisation and Allied Breweries. These were the 'chartered users'. Each agreed to pay 80 per cent of the purchase price for their systems in advance of delivery, in return for favourable pricing terms. In addition the Department of Industry provided another £25,000 or so in the form of a development grant. By the spring of 1979 Xionics was ready to roll.

The first prototype XIBUS was demonstrated in May 1980. After a few bugs had been ironed out, production of systems for the chartered users began. These were developed in two stages: stage 1 systems worked but they involved only partial duplication of the network and control equipment. Full duplication, involving extensive software development, was to come later with stage 2.

Between November 1980 and April 1981, stage 1 systems were installed with the chartered users. They went down well and led to orders for further equipment and facilities. During 1980 Xionics received its first order on commercial terms from ICI's Mond Division on Merseyside. The Mond System involved the linking of some 40 Xionics multi-function work stations, an IBM mainframe computer, a large DEC 10 Minicomputer, word-processors and the Telex network to provide automated office facilities at four sites. A stage 1 system was installed in April 1981 and trial use of the ICI XIBUS began shortly afterwards.

It is hard to overestimate the significance of the ICI contract. The company turned out to be a near-perfect customer. The Mond people appeared to understand almost immediately the power of XIBUS and they went about its introduction in an enlightened and imaginative way. They could have up to 3,000 users linked to the system eventually.

Meanwhile, Xionics itself was experiencing growth pains. After completion of the stage 1 installations, the company had to gear up for full-scale production. Bevan persuaded the Department of Industry to part with another £200,000 but it was clear that more cash would be needed.

In December 1980 a capital restructuring took place. Meritor Investments, a venture-capital company owned jointly by Midland Bank and the Rolls-Royce pension fund, bought a 25.1 per cent equity stake from Multihavens and then subscribed for £240,000 worth of preference shares backed up by £225,000 of loans. In addition, Multihavens subscribed for £60,000 of preference shares to support its remaining 14.9 per cent equity holding. Bevan was left with 51 per cent of the company with the remaining 9 per cent going to his chief collaborator and colleague, Ian Richardson.

The new company's reputation was further enhanced early in 1981 by an order from Kenneth Baker, Minister for Information Technology, for £250,000 worth of XIBUS equipment to be installed in the Cabinet Office as the first of a number of government-sponsored 'electronic office' projects.

Soon afterwards a small pilot production facility was opened at Letchworth. It was operating efficiently enough by the end of 1981 to begin production of the equipment needed to upgrade stage 1 systems to stage 2. Early in 1982 the first phase of the Cabinet Office system was installed on schedule. It was formally accepted in April of that year.

Mike Bevan's instinct about DATABUS has proved sound. At a time of important structural change in computer technology, characterised by the advent of networking which is itself a response to a wider distribution of computing within organisations, the idea of a completely open systems architecture has proved a powerful one.

The provision in the XIBUS design for the use of optical fibres as the communicating medium, instead of the more limited coaxial cable, is another important feature. Bevan is convinced that fibre optics, which use digital transmission methods, will be 'the dominant transmission technology of the 1980s'. He predicts that 'All the alternatives' (and that includes the putative industry standard, ETHERNET, developed by Xerox Corporation) 'are doomed to failure.'

It is clear from this that nothing has happened during the past eight years or so to diminish in any way Bevan's original conviction that he was on to a commercial winner. A customer once said of XIBUS, 'If IBM had this system they would go for 99% of the world business systems market.' And there lies the rub. XIBUS was a big idea locked up in a small company. It needed to be marketed heavily all over the world if the lead that Xionics had established was not to melt away. That is why, in late-1982, Mike Bevan began to contemplate the idea of reaping his entrepreneurial reward. He had contracted the wish by then to make a spectacular entry into the all-important American market in 1983 and he was aware that Xionics itself, though profitable by then, was not generating enough cash to finance such an adventure.

In addition, he took the view that to enter a new market it was essential, however good the technology, to have a big name behind you, capable of deploying substantial marketing muscle. He felt he was faced with two choices. Sell the company to a large British group (the DoI, having funded much of the development work, would have had the right and probably the inclination to veto an overseas buyer) or bring in new venture-capital partners who had sufficiently good US contacts to arrange an effective transfer of the technology across the Atlantic.

When I spoke to Mike Bevan in late-1982 he had not decided which of these options to choose. It was clear by then, however, that he would not agonise long over the prospect of surrendering control of Xionics. 'I've changed,' he said. 'I like running an organisation. And the money side is not unimportant. I give the idea of becoming a multi-millionaire the odd spot of thought.'

The speed with which Xionics has established itself in what is expected to become a huge market, but one which is ostensibly dominated by large companies, is something of a puzzle for those who subscribe to the conventional wisdoms of corporate economics.

Theoretically it should not have happened. Entry costs are high in the business-equipment market. New products are supposed to absorb vast amounts of R&D funding for both hardware and software. IBM spent hundreds of millions of dollars in the early 1960s on developing its hugely successful 360 series of computers.

One reason why Xionics has succeeded is that Mike Bevan's thinking about business systems was less constrained than that of his rivals working in the large companies. He saw the problem and then the solution more clearly because his vision was not obscured by commitments to existing markets or concern about an existing customer base.

Perhaps even more important was his readiness to listen to what the users were saying. When business technology took off at the beginning of the 1960s, the scientists moved into the driving seat and began pushing along their own development paths. They lost the habit of listening to what their customers were saying. 'Technology Push' was substituted for 'Market Pull'. Users were told not to worry; something ten times better, costing half as much would be along tomorrow. Such tunnel vision was bound to catch up with the big companies in the end. There had to come a time when the difference between what was wanted and what was available was substantial enough to represent a new market.

All that was needed were the ears to hear what users were

saying and the technical ability to interpret the information and work out a way of building a product round it. That is the essence of the inspiration on which Xionics was founded. The story of Xionics might, perhaps, be interpreted as evidence to support a view quite contrary to my 'Dinosaur & Co' thesis. After all, in this case at least, the small size and agility that I make so much of were not sufficient to enable Xionics to break into the US market on its own. Mike Bevan felt the need for more substantial support. Does this not suggest that large companies will continue to have a role in the exploitation of high technology and thus will not be forced to disintegrate?

There are two reasons to doubt this. In the first place, the marketing and financial 'muscle', which Mike Bevan felt the lack of when plotting his onslaught on the American market, need not always be the exclusive prerogatives of the large companies. It is not hard to imagine, when the disintegration process has progressed apace, the emergence of more sophisticated capital markets, capable of assessing the worth of projects like XIBUS and of mustering the necessary financial and marketing back-up. Indeed, muscles of the financial and marketing kinds are eminently suitable cases for 'unbundling'. Venture-capital companies, employing 'hands-on' investment policies, together with specialist marketing consultancies, should be capable of performing these roles quite independently of the large companies.

In the second place, Xionics is an unusual company. It was created specifically for the exploitation of DATABUS. Mike Bevan's first company was very different in this respect. It was established as a generally competent service company, not as a vehicle for a particular product. Unlike Xionics, M. J. Bevan Ltd was its own *raison d'être*.

I suggested to Mike Bevan that he sets more store now by the commercialisation of a technical idea than he does by the survival as an independent entity of the company he created. He replied that this was the case 'if and only if the two are mutually exclusive'.

That they may sometimes be mutually exclusive suggests that the traditional association between the entrepreneur and his/her company is not quite adequate. There seems also to be an important link between the entrepreneur and his/her product.

Which link is dominant, whether the company or the brain-child bond, will only become apparent if they ever come into conflict. I suspect such conflicts are rare and, for the reasons I have already mentioned, I expect them to become rarer.

Epilogue

In May 1983 it was announced that Smiths Industries, the large electronics and instrumentation group now engaged in reducing its former dependence on the motor industry, had acquired 95 per cent of Xionics. The initial consideration was £600,000, but this will rise to several millions of pounds if a number of quite conservative performance targets are met. Mike Bevan retains a 4 per cent stake in the company and Ian Richardson is left with 1 per cent.

Bevan was attracted to Smiths for a number of reasons, some positive, some negative. Smiths offered the international marketing strength Bevan believes XIBUS badly needs if it is to exploit to the full the window of opportunity represented by its technological lead. Another attraction was that Smiths has developed in recent years great expertise and competence in microelectronics which could aid Xionics in its scramble for world prominence during the second half of the 1980s.

On the negative side, Smiths had, until its acquisition of Xionics, no presence at all in the rapidly growing business equipment market. There was thus no pre-existing structure into which Smiths might have been tempted to mould Xionics. Bevan will be the group's leading expert in the field and there seems a good chance that he will, as a consequence, be invited to join the main board in the not too distant future – that is always assuming that he decides to stay after his five-year contract expires.

6
Dr Hermann Hauser, Chris Curry and Acorn Computers

One of the most important areas of economic activity in Britain over the next two decades will be the area around the dividing line (what computer people would call the 'interface') between the business and academic establishments.

If we are to perform well in the era of rapid technological change (ERTA), we must be capable not only of generating good technology, but also of shaping it into marketable products. There is no magic formula for ensuring that all useful, university-generated technology is automatically transformed into marketable product. The transfer can and does take place in many different ways. In the end, though, it usually boils down to a matter of personal contact. An effective way of establishing and maintaining such contact is for academics and businessmen to form companies together.

A good example of this kind of partnership is the team of Prof. Herbert Boyer and Mr Bob Swanson, a scientist and an entrepreneur, who have together built one of the world's leading biotechnology companies, Genentech of Cupertino, California.

Another example, closer to home, is the team of Dr Hermann Hauser and Mr Chris Curry, who are together building one of the world's most promising computer companies, Acorn Computers of Cambridge, England. Hermann Hauser was born in Vienna on 23 October 1948, the son of a Viennese mother and a wealthy Tyrolean wine distributor. The family settled in the Tyrol, where the children were educated at both primary and secondary levels. At the age of 15 Hermann was despatched by his father to Cambridge to learn English; 'It is important to learn languages', said his father, 'and English is the most important language.'

Hermann thoroughly enjoyed the visit. He was impressed by the British, and says central Europeans, from more regimented societies, are often surprised by the British style of non-interference and their tolerance of eccentricity. French being the second most important language, there was a trip to Paris in the summer of Hermann's seventeenth year, but next time he persuaded his father to allow him to return to Cambridge. This time Hermann studied Russian, as much to mix with English students and improve his English as to learn yet another language.

Hauser achieved his 'matura', the equivalent of our 'A' levels but much less specialised, and went to Vienna University to read theoretical physics. He lived initially with his grandmother and then later, after her death, with his aunt. He was a rather pampered student but was none the less industrious and intellectually active.

In addition to his interest in physics he became fascinated by developments in genetics and particularly by the fine, popularising book *Chance and Necessity* by the French Nobel laureate, Jacques Monod. He had become at the age of 19 a self-acknowledged intellectual, arranging meetings of like-minded students at his Vienna home to discuss the important issues of the day. As well as gravity waves and Monod's 'operon', the topics discussed included the more typically Viennese issues raised by Rudolph Carnap and the logical positivists of the Vienna Circle.

After three busy years, Hauser graduated with the equivalent of a first class degree in Physics and looked well on the way to a promising academic career. During the degree course, Hauser used to return to Cambridge to work as a summer research assistant at the Cavendish Laboratory. In Vienna the physics was very theoretical. There was not the money for elaborate experiments of the kind theoretical physicists were demanding and anyway, as with music, the Viennese style was, on the whole, passive. Physicists there preferred to play around with ideas rather than cyclotrons; they were reluctant to get their hands dirty. The British built things at the Cavendish. Hauser himself worked on high-speed photography and powerful lasers, amongst other things.

His trips to Cambridge were the passport he needed to the university and after he graduated he was offered a place at King's College to prepare for a PhD. The ingredients of the four years at King's were similar to what had gone before: an industrious application to the task at hand, much stimulating discussion with gifted friends and colleagues, intermingled with tennis and frequent punting trips up and down the Cam. The subject of Hauser's PhD thesis was a new computerised analysis of experimental data obtained with a thermobalance and a differential scanning calorimeter.

In Cambridge, the tradition is that if you need a computer you have to learn how to use it. So it was that Hermann Hauser began to haunt the Computer Laboratory, becoming increasingly fascinated by the hardware, the sort of people who worked there and by the kind of reasoning the IBM 370 machine demanded of them. He learned the computer language Fortran and he believes he was one of the first in the Cavendish to bind computer-plotter output into his thesis.

The next step seemed more or less automatic – post-doctoral work at the Cavendish. But then Hauser began to have doubts about what he was doing with his life. He decided there were two options open to him: one, to complete his post-doctoral project and try to win a place as a lecturer; two, to return to Austria and help his father run the family wine business.

He was quite attracted to the idea of running a business but he felt that his PhD would not be very useful in the wine industry – it seemed a bit of a waste and he knew that if he went back he would miss Cambridge dreadfully. Whilst he was musing about the destiny of Hermann Hauser it became apparent that his friend Chris Curry was also at a turning point.

Curry had arrived at the crossroads by quite a different route. He was born in Cambridge on 28 January 1946 and educated at St Neots nearby and then at a minor public school at Kimbolton where he obtained 'A' levels in maths and physics. He flirted for a while with the idea of going to Southampton University but he was anxious to be paid while he was completing his education. In 1964 he joined Pye, the Cambridge electronics group, as a student apprentice. Amongst other things he perfected the soldering techniques he had been employing, from an early age, as a keen hobbyist. He left Pye after a few months to join the Royal Radar Establishment at Malvern, working on radar for the ill-fated TSR2 bomber project and on 'super-conducting junctions' (crossed wires immersed in a bath of liquid helium).

Malvern was and remains at the leading-edge of technology. It was there that Professor Dummer first suggested the idea of the integrated circuit and where Messrs Toby and Dinsdale developed the first transistor amplifier. Curry enjoyed his time at the RRE but he never settled. He left after nine months to join ITT's W.R. Grace research laboratories where he worked on electronic measuring equipment. He spent six months at Grace, still unsure about whether his life should develop along technical or literary lines. He was very interested in computers by then, but he was reading a great deal of science-fiction and was tempted to try his hand at writing.

Then, in mid-1966, he and a friend from W. R. Grace spotted an advertisement for engineers placed by Clive Sinclair, then on the point of leaving London to set up a new base for his company Sinclair Radionics in Cambridge. Curry and his friend applied for the job and were both hired. Sinclair's products at the time, sold through mail order mostly to the hobby market, included radios and amplifiers. The new Z range of amplifiers came out soon after Curry's arrival, and he worked long hours on Sinclair's miniature TV project, winding deflection coils with hair-thin wires. The coils needed 2,500 turns and Curry remembers that after 1,500 turns, one either broke the wire or lost count. The first miniature TV was shown at the Radio Show in 1966 and caused quite a stir. There was a long way to go yet, however, before it reached production.

Hi-Fi was doing well, though, in those days especially the new series 2000 and 3000 boxed systems. This was the brief hey-day of the British Hi-Fi industry, before the Japanese arrived. And then Clive Sinclair returned from a trip to the States with a sample of the world's first calculator on a chip, just developed by Texas Instruments, and a bundle of papers. He appointed Chris Curry leader of a development project which was to culminate in 1971 with the launch of the world's first working, single-chip calculator. It was called the Sinclair 'Executive' and it retailed for £79. It was honoured with a place in the Museum of Modern Art in New York

Entry into the calculator market led to a massive expansion of Sinclair's business. A production line was set up at St Ives outside Cambridge and a whole family of calculators was developed, including the Sinclair Cambridge, the Sinclair Oxford and finally the up-market Sovereigns, the production of whose metal cases was subcontracted to a pen-nib manufacturer.

But the fully-integrated Japanese electronics companies, making chips and calculators, soon moved strongly into the market with their Liquid Crystal Display (LCD) calculators. Sinclair responded by developing the Black Watch which would have been the world's first, mass-produced electronic wristwatch, had Sinclair Radionics not been let down badly by its original chip supplier.

That delay and the product's notorious unreliability caused Sinclair to seek outside funding for his still cherished TV project. The National Enterprise Board took an equity stake in Radionics in 1974. The partnership proved less than harmonious and in 1976 Sinclair suggested to Curry that they set up a separate company, called Science of Cambridge. SoC, run initially as a one-man band by Chris, was an instant success. Its first product was a wrist calculator sold in kit-form by mail order for £9. It generated revenues of over £250,000 and was highly profitable.

Sinclair and Curry toyed for a while with the idea of making a reflecting telescope for amateur astronomers, but then Curry's attention was caught by an advertisement in a US hobbyist magazine for a 'computer-in-a-book'. He asked around Cambridge how one should go about making such a product and began approaching suppliers. US chip-maker National Semiconductor suggested they should make a machine based on a set of NS parts. Clive Sinclair was persuaded and he gave the project the go ahead.

The result was a rudimentary computer called MK14 which was first exhibited in the spring of 1977. It was a huge success. It used a calculator display and sold, again by mail order, for £39.95. It was programmable in 'hexadecimal' and was bought in large numbers both by hobbyists and by companies as an early development tool for the new breed of microprocessors.

It was during the incubation of the MK14 that Curry began to see quite a bit of Hermann Hauser whom he had known since the Austrian first came to Cambridge to learn Russian. They discussed all sorts of ideas for business ventures, including the invention and marketing of a new craze game.

Meanwhile the MK14 was still arousing interest, particularly from companies anxious to explore microprocessor technology for their own businesses. Sinclair was not inclined to follow up these inquiries, so in 1978 Curry and Hauser formed CPU Ltd. (CPU are the initials of a computer's Central Processing Unit and in this context they stand for Cambridge Processing Unit.)

The purpose of the company was to follow up those MK14 inquiries. Hauser had helped during the development of the MK14 and he shared Curry's enthusiasm for the new technology. To complement Curry's long experience in production engineering, project management, parts procurement, pricing and mail-order marketing, Hauser brought to the partnership excellent contacts within Cambridge University.

But for the time being CPU remained for Curry in 'background mode', as he puts it. He continued to work at SoC, urging Sinclair to follow up the success of the MK14 with a more powerful version which could be programmed in the high-level language, BASIC. In the end Sinclair agreed, but he decided to pursue the Super-MK14 within Radionics. Curry believes that had the project come to fruition there, Sinclair would probably have made enough money to exercise options he held to buy back control of Radionics from the NEB. As it was, the NEB decided it was an unsuitable venture for Radionics and they whisked it away to another of their companies, Newbury Laboratories. It re-emerged some years later as the 'Newbrain' computer.

Meanwhile, Sinclair's relationship with the NEB reached a low ebb. He abandoned Radionics and retreated to his SoC lifeboat. Curry decided it was time to leave and, six months after its formation, he joined CPU full time. CPU's first contract, completed while Curry was still at SoC, came from a Welsh fruit-machine manufacturer and was worth £3,000. The new company's working capital requirements were entirely financed by a £1,000 front-end payment for this project.

The task was to re-engineer the electro-mechanical innards of fruit machines along electronic lines. Hauser reckons the customer got a very good deal. He believes the CPU work must have been one of the cheapest fully-grown microprocessor systems ever completed.

In those early days CPU was a three-man band. There was Hauser, Curry and Chris Turner who had been Hauser's research assistant at the Cavendish. There were also two Cambridge University men in at the beginning, aerodynamicist Dr Stephen Furber and computer scientist Roger Wilson.

A third academic, Dr Andy Hopper – later to become a director of Acorn Computers – had earlier formed a company with Hermann Hauser called Orbis Ltd to exploit the 'Cambridge Ring' networking technology Hopper had developed at the university. Orbis later became an Acorn subsidiary. CPU's and Acorn's access to the Cambridge Computer Lab and their friendly relations with some of the talented people who work there has proved extremely useful.

There was never any formal arrangement. The university was, in principle, favourably disposed towards the idea of helping out small firms in the Cambridge area. No permissions were granted, however, and no formal system of encouragement was established. It was an example of that peculiarly English kind of tolerance that had attracted Hermann Hauser to Cambridge in the first place.

CPU/Acorn was not the only outfit to benefit from the Computer Lab's 'open door' policy. There are dozens of small computer companies working in the Cambridge area all with links of varying intimacy with the university. Thanks largely to the catalytic influence of a young banker called Matthew Bullock and Jack Long of a company called Topexpress, the Cambridge Computer Group was formed in 1979 to represent these companies and to discuss matters of mutual interest. When money began to get tight for the Computer Lab in late 1981, the university approached the group suggesting that its members might contribute some cash in return for their access to university facilities and personnel. The members agreed to do so immediately and now they have *de jure* as well as *de facto* access to the boffins and their electronic brains.

In practice the links still work much as they ever did. In the early days of CPU the idea was for Curry or Hauser to go out and win the business, bring the contract specification back and take a long, hard look at it as a collection of engineering problems.

Having broken the job down into its discrete parts, Hauser would then get on the phone to his friends at the university and find out who the experts were in the relevant areas. The experts were then invited round for a cup of tea and a chat. It became, after a while, a normal part of academic life. One would be working away on a thesis or a programming problem and a colleague would put his head round the corner and say 'Hermann Hauser's on the phone and would like a word if you've got a moment.'

Probably it was quite refreshing to consult for people who appreciated your special skills, and the fees earned must have come in handy too. I do not suppose it occurred to the students that they were crossing a threshold dividing two very different fields of endeavour. CPU turned over £23,559 worth of business in the year to mid-1979 and earned a modest but promising £2,693 in profit.

But the young entrepreneurs began to find it irksome to dream up and develop excellent new products for their customers, so they began to look around for a product of their own. The first idea was for an electronic diary. They went to their software ace Roger Wilson with the proposition.

Wilson said he could do that easily enough and added, more or less by the by, that he had read a review of the MK14 and had just designed a much better version which he called 'HAWK'. Hauser was intrigued and Curry was already feeling frustrated at SoC by his inability to work on an MK14 follow up. It was agreed that the diary would keep while the idea of the HAWK was investigated. Three days later Wilson came back with the machine wired up on a 'breadboard' (an experimental prototype). The instructions or 'software' needed to make the computer work took the form of a program of 512 'bytes' (a byte is a group of binary digits which operate as one unit).

Before the rig could be tested, this program had to be incorporated into a chip called a PROM (Programmable Read-Only Memory). Hauser arranged to 'blow' the PROM knowing full well that it would not be quite as easy as that. A 512-byte program written in machine code was bound to have some bugs in it which would need to be sorted out before the Wilson contraption could hope to work.

Roger Wilson was more sanguine. He was in the second year of his degree course and full of youthful confidence in his own ability. He said, 'It's going to work.' It did, straight away. There were three minor bugs but they were easy to correct because the device as a whole ran. Hauser was enormously impressed. He remembers thinking, 'This guy knows what he's about.' A year later, when Roger Wilson graduated, he joined Acorn full-time. Since then he has written two full computer languages for Acorn products – 'Atom' BASIC and 'BBC' BASIC – virtually single-handed (BASIC is the most widely used language on microcomputers and is an acronym for Beginners' All-purpose Symbolic Instruction Code).

Acorn Computers Ltd was formed as a separate company in March 1979. Wilson's HAWK, re-christened 'System 1', was its first product. It was sold by mail order and is still selling. At £70 it was more expensive than the £40 MK14, but it was more powerful, could be upgraded to run in BASIC and was fully expandable. Expansion 'cards' were the obvious diversification route from System 1. Altogether Acorn developed 24 'Eurocard'-sized circuit boards which could be slotted into System 1 to make it do different things. It was clear by mid-1979 that Hauser and Curry had found a slot in the hobby computer market which they were capable of filling competently and profitably. But then the pace began to quicken.

Newbury Laboratories announced that on the basis of the super-MK14 project they had inherited from Radionics, they would be launching within six months a cased, single-board computer, ready to run, aimed at a market that would be considerably larger than the hardcore hobby market at which System 1 and the MK14 had been targeted.

The machine was to be called the 'Newbrain' and its specification looked both impressive and eminently feasible. Whether Newbury Labs were wise to disclose their plans in such detail is open to doubt. The revelation accelerated development throughout the embryonic UK micro-computer industry.

At the same time it was rumoured that Clive Sinclair, now back full-time at SoC, was also working on a cheap, single-board machine. It was clear to those involved in this part of the industry that there was money to be made here. However, it is one thing to spot a market opportunity and quite another to develop a competitive product in a hurry. It is not just a question of sticking a few standard chips onto a printed circuit board, wiring them up and then placing advertisements.

Chips have to be cajoled with subtly designed software into doing what is required of them. As Hermann Hauser puts it, 'The trick is to fit the chips together so that they make a harmonious whole. You have to balance hardware against software; features against price.'

Acorn decided to enter the race. Hauser and Curry had been thinking about single-board computers for some time, but the 'Newbrain' announcement was what got them going. In the event the Acorn 'Atom' and the Sinclair 'ZX80' appeared more or less simultaneously. The Newbrain was nowhere to be seen. It was beset by problems and only finally emerged in mid-1982.

The task of gearing up for the Atom – the first of a series of Acorn products to be named after the *dramatis personae* of Hauser's first intellectual love, nuclear physics – sent the entrepreneur round the world. Hauser flew first to Washington to arrange a deal for the Atom's keyboard, and then to California, to the giant Rockwell International, to fix up supplies of the Atom's heart, the 6502 micro-processor. Hauser wanted about 5,000 of them and he wanted 30 days' credit. Normally, in deals involving relatively unknown foreign companies, the likes of Rockwell would demand a letter of credit from its new customer until the two parties got to know each other well enough for an ordinary account to be opened. But fortune smiled. The picture of the Atom prototype Hauser had with him caught the fancy of the Rockwell people and they opened an account for Acorn straight away.

Last stop was Hong Kong to finalise a deal on the Atom's case Chris Curry had fixed up earlier. The two men were quite confident about the Atom at this stage. The development costs were not high; they estimated that they would make a profit on the project if they sold 1,000 of them. To date they have sold about 30,000 Atoms.

The company's finances during this period were straightforward. There was money coming in from the consultancy work, System 1 and the Eurocards. The overdraft facility Hauser had negotiated at the outset helped to smooth cash-flow.

Hauser had been with National Westminster Bank while a student and it seemed natural to go there when he decided to set up in business. He told the manager he was starting a company with an experienced partner and said he wanted a £5,000 overdraft facility. The manager, impressed by the business plan and perhaps re-assured by Hauser's recently acquired 'Certified Diploma of Accounting and Finance', said fine and suggested he come back in a month or so to report how the business was going. Hauser took the manager at his word and returned a few weeks later with a progress report and a request that the facility be increased to £10,000. Once again the manager said 'Fine'. It was as easy as that.

The fact that the company's account kept going into the black each month as the business developed probably helped to sustain the manager's equable and helpful attitude. There were no scares or sudden surges in the overdraft; it must have seemed to the banker that Hauser and Curry knew what they were about and were building up their business with the right mixture of opportunism and prudence.

It was not long before the Atom took up the running from System 1 and the Eurocards. It appealed to a much larger market. Unlike its chief rival the Sinclair ZX80, it had a proper keyboard and was extremely expandable with the simple, plug-in addition of extra cards to provide more memory and extra facilities. In addition the Atom has its own version of BASIC written by Roger Wilson. It is rather odd compared to other variants of BASIC such as 'Dartmouth' or 'Microsoft' but it uses the 6502's processing power economically, or 'elegantly' as they would say in the trade, conferring on the Atom (the basic machine cost £150) an impressive price/performance ratio.

During the summer of 1980, when the Atom was firmly established and beginning to sell in large numbers, Hauser and Curry began to think about the next step. The business was looking healthy enough, but if one thing was obvious about the microcomputer industry by then, it was that you could not afford to rest on your laurels.

Not only were new devices like the 16-bit processor being developed, but the price of existing parts was constantly falling, opening up new possibilities and posing new competitive threats.

From the beginning, Hauser and Curry have gained much strength from the Cambridge Computer Lab. Their access to the resident genii there enabled them to expand System 1 into the pricier Systems 2–5 for the educational and government markets, at the same time opening up new market areas for the Atom which could be used in conjunction with the more sophisticated versions of System 1. In addition, the remarkably gifted Andy Hopper, now a fellow of Corpus Christi college and an assistant lecturer at the university, had introduced Hauser and Curry to networking technology through Orbis. Hopper was joint recipient of the 1981 British Computer Society Award for outstanding achievement. The prize honoured the Cambridge Ring project, an innovative Local Area Network system which Acorn soon began to sell to universities, government and a number of companies.

And there was also the ECONET, a communication system designed specifically for low-cost computers like the Atom and sold mainly into the educational market. Networking is a technology of the first importance, and as early as 1980, it was within the mainstream of Acorn's product development strategy. The market Curry and Hauser had their sights on was computers and computer systems costing under £1,000. With the Atom they had begun at the bottom of that market: the general idea was to build on that and move upwards, to launch a frontal attack on the market leaders, Commodore and Apple. Networking systems and the more sophisticated variants of System 1 were ways of increasing the potential of the Atom, but some sort of super-Atom was needed as a basis for Acorn's next quantum jump.

And so, in October 1980, twelve people convened for a meeting at the company's offices in Bridge Street, Cambridge. Hauser says it was the most extraordinary meeting he has ever attended. The main protagonists were Stephen Furber, Roger Wilson, Andy Hopper, Chris Curry and Hermann Hauser.

It was clear from the beginning that agreement was not to be hoped for; there were too many conflicting ideas about what the super-Atom should be. Furber wanted the next product to be a single processor machine, Wilson was insisting on a dual processor arrangement, Hopper was anxious for Acorn to move into 16-bit processor technology and Curry, his eyes firmly on the marketplace, was demanding that the product should not cost more than £300. Hauser had an equally vain wish – he wanted to prevent the meeting from turning into a brawl.

The importance of the no-brawl result lay in the unusually comprehensive nature of the Acorn design team. The company has its own hardware experts which is quite normal in a computer-producing concern; much less usual is that it also has 'in-house' software experts led by Roger Wilson and 'in-house' network experts led by Andy Hopper; uniquely, it has an 'in-house' ability to design its own chips. Other companies just develop the logic circuits for their chips – they get outside specialists to transfer the logic circuits onto the chip itself.

This well-rounded quality of the Acorn team is extremely precious. As Hauser says, 'It means you immediately get an answer about whether something is possible.' Hauser was fearful that if a brawl did develop the integrity of the team might be at risk; umbrage might be taken, disappointment might turn into resentment, people might leave and some of them might never come back. All the ingredients were there in those mutually exclusive requirements.

In the event Cambridge came to the diplomat's aid; or rather the spirit of Cambridge, the extraordinary intellectual arrogance the place engenders. Instead of beginning immediately with the laborious task of working out a compromise which would leave everyone disappointed but no one unduly so, the meeting decided first to entertain the idea of meeting all the requirements.

A number of proposals were bandied back and forth with Curry busily working out the market implications each time. The discussion began to converge on a single chip that did not exist – a device that came to be known as the 'TUBE'. It had magical properties; it could permit 8-bit, 16-bit or 32-bit, or any other sort of processors for that matter, to talk to each other, it would be quite cheap and above all, it would achieve the desired no-brawl result to the meeting. It would do more than that – it would permit everyone to leave the meeting with more than they had been asking for.

The question was, granted that the TUBE could do all these things, granted that it was conceivable, could it be made? Was the TUBE, like the ever-lasting light bulb, a good idea in theory but quite impossible to realise? If any group of people in the world could have answered that question, they were probably at that meeting. They said it was possible, though whether they were certain of that when they said it is doubtful. But in Cambridge, if you say something is possible, people expect you to prove it.

After the Bridge Street brainstorming session work was begun on fleshing out the product idea that had emerged. The new machine, which was to be called the 'Proton' (a sub-atomic particle one step down the microcosmic scale from the Atom), was, in theory at least, extraordinarily expandable – a quality that has been evident to an unusual degree in all Acorn products to date.

You started off with a conventional 8-bit single processor machine with an impressive array of ports at the back, including the magic TUBE. You could then add, at will, extra memory, a second 8-bit processor, a 16-bit or a 32-bit. It meant that the basic machine could eventually become the nucleus of an extremely powerful 32-bit microcomputer, quite capable of mounting a strong attack on the business systems market. But the Bridge Street ideas were, in the end, realised in another product.

The BBC, becoming conscious of their power to inform and educate, had decided some two years previously to put together a series of TV programmes on computer literacy. When they heard about the 'Newbrain' computer to be launched in mid-1980, they went to Newbury Laboratories and suggested the 'Newbrain' should become the official BBC computer, through which the TV series would be conducted. Newbury Labs agreed to this proposal with alacrity.

But Chris Curry bridled at the idea of a potentially huge contract being awarded on the equivalent of a single-tender basis by a state-owned broadcasting organisation to the subsidiary of a state-owned investment company, the NEB. He persuaded a number of fellow computer-makers, including Clive Sinclair, to write to the BBC to complain.

Towards the end of 1980 the BBC, becoming concerned about the delays in the 'Newbrain' development schedule, agreed to throw the competition open. Both Acorn and Sinclair Research (the re-named SoC) went for it. Acorn received its first visit from a two-man BBC team on a Monday in January 1981. Hauser and Curry were told, more or less precisely, what the BBC wanted. It was agreed that they should meet again on the following Friday to see how digestible Acorn had found the specifications.

The BBC had evolved their specifications over a two-year planning period and quite independently of what was happening in the industry. If, by pure chance, a company's product development was progressing along lines compatible with BBC thinking, then that company would clearly have an important edge in the competition over its less fortunate rivals. And so it was with Acorn. The Atom had the right sort of keyboard, it could handle colour and it had networking capabilities. The Proton, which was still on the drawing-board then, was even closer to the BBC specification and promised an even better price/performance ratio than the BBC were asking for.

After that first meeting on the Monday Hauser was convinced that here was a major opportunity for the company. Quite by accident, much of the early work had already been done. 'How', he asked himself, 'do we exploit this advantage?' He was aware that following the saga of the Newbrain, the BBC men were very sensitive about time. Hauser reckoned that they would be impressed by a company that could come up with clever ideas AND get a prototype working quickly.

And so Hauser determined on a bold endeavour. He decided to try to get a prototype together before the BBC men returned on Friday. That evening he rang up software expert Roger Wilson and put to him the idea of a Friday morning deadline for a breadboard prototype. Wilson laughed incredulously and said 'quite impossible' or, rather, less polite words to that effect. So Hauser rang up hardware ace Stephen Furber, and said that Roger Wilson thought it might just be possible to get a rig together in time for the scheduled meeting with the BBC people. Furber also laughed the idea out of court. But in the end, both

Furber and Wilson agreed to give it a try. There was, after all, nothing to lose apart from a few nights' sleep. Wilson says of Hauser's deviousness, 'We was framed!!'

Hauser started phoning again to gather together the talents needed for the crash programme. The invitation this time was not 'How about dropping round for a cup of tea?' but 'How about dropping everything for two days and helping us put together a working model of a completely new computer by Friday morning?'

The Computer Lab people responded. Perhaps the most significant phone call, in view of the time problem, was to a young Indian postgraduate, Ramanuj Benerji. Ramanuj had established a reputation in the Computer Lab as an extremely quick and skilful 'wire-wrapper' – the person who links all the elements of an electronic device together, working from a wiring diagram. 'We went to the fastest gun in the West', says Hauser. After gaining his PhD in October 1982, Ramanuj Benerji joined Acorn full time.

On Friday, 8.00 a.m., the design team gathered at Bridge Street with the product of two days and three nights of intense effort. It was the skeleton of a high-speed, 32K microcomputer. It didn't work. It should have, according to the plans, but the BBC team were due in a couple of hours and the damned thing didn't work. They tried everything but there wasn't a 'cheep' out of the thing. They were beginning to think that there was some serious design fault somewhere when Hermann Hauser, an entrepreneur now rather than an engineer, made a tentative suggestion. He said that perhaps there was a problem with the internal clock which all computers need. The breadboard rig was using the clock of a System 3 board lying nearby – Hauser suggested this might be introducing phase errors into the new computer. So they switched over to the computer's own clock and lo and behold, it ran. The BBC men were very impressed. Several weeks later it was announced that Acorn had won the BBC micro-computer contract.

The Acorn team were cock-a-hoop. Nothing seemed impossible. The confident impetus carried them casually over a substantial technical obstacle encountered in the spring of 1981. It was to do with the design of the computer's circuit board. The logic circuits had all been mapped out and tested, but when all the integrated circuits were added up, it looked as if the machine was going to need about 200 chips – far too many for the size of the machine contemplated.

Chip economy could be bought with the use of a special sort of chip called an Uncommitted Logic Array (ULA), but this would require a long and painstaking ULA design period which could easily inject serious delays into an already tight development schedule. It was a toss up between going for a much larger board than Acorn really wanted, or taking a gamble on the ULA route.

It so happened that Andy Hopper was working in the Computer Lab on a set of software tools which, if they worked, would greatly speed up the process of ULA design. Hauser and Curry decided to gamble on the Hopper toolkit. They had faith in Hopper and his team, including Jeremy Dion and Peter Robinson, and though Andy himself admits to a few sleepless nights when he despaired of cracking the problems, that faith was rewarded. But the ULA was not finished with Acorn yet.

It was in August 1981 when the first sample of 12 ULA chips arrived from the manufacturer, Ferranti. The whole team watched anxiously as they were plugged into a development prototype, hoping against hope that this, the most ambitious of the custom chips in the computer, would work as well when etched into a sliver of silicon as it had on the drawing board. It did. There was much cheering and merrymaking. Hauser disappeared and came back with a bottle of champagne. All 12 of the initial sample checked out perfectly. They were in business.

When, out of a sample of 12 chips, 12 work then the customer can be excused for feeling confident that the 'yield' on production batches is going to be high. But that sample batch of 12 turned out to be a statistical freak. Of the 3,000 chips in the first production batch, about 2,600 were useless. They worked all right but they were too slow at handling the computer's video display. This technical problem, which could be solved simply enough by tinkering around with the circuit design and the production process – a trial and error procedure known as 'iteration' – led to serious financial consequences.

While the development work had been approaching its conclusion, Acorn had been busily gearing up for full-scale production due to start in December 1981. This involved placing orders for components like cases and keyboards, arranging final assembly, supplying sub-contractors with all the bits and pieces and generally investing substantial amounts of pre-production working capital.

By the launch in January, production was supposed to be up to 5,000 machines a month. The ULA iterations messed up the schedule completely and in the absence of revenue from sales at the expected date, the company's overdraft began to soar. Hauser went along to the bank, now with a new manager, and explained the situation. He asked for a substantial increase in the overdraft facility while the production difficulties were sorted out. The manager said he would think about it. Three weeks later, having heard nothing, Hauser decided to explore other avenues.

Barclays Bank had been courting Acorn for three years and through Matthew Bullock (by then departed for London) and Walter Herriot, both of whom had been involved in the formation of the Cambridge Computer Group, they knew the company well. Hauser explained his problem to Barclays and within a week agreement on adequate overdraft facilities had been reached. Acorn switched its bank account. Barclays was keen to introduce Acorn to its subsidiary Barclays Merchant Bank when the company became a little larger, but there was no obligation on Acorn to go to BMB. It was a straightforward branch banking arrangement that was agreed in early 1982 between a company in temporary financial difficulties and a bank with sufficient vision to see that the problems would be temporary.

In the event the launch of the BBC computer was delayed for six weeks while the ULA iterations were completed. Hauser and Curry are grateful not only to Barclays for providing the financial cushion but also to their suppliers who were very understanding and particularly to Ferranti which agreed to support the cost of the iterations and to press ahead with the procedure at top speed.

The BBC computer was always going to be a low-margin, high-volume product for Acorn, sold through mail order at rock bottom prices. The machines were so powerful, however – they offered so much more than the BBC had bargained for – that

1. David Murray of Sera-Lab in May 1981. By then he was already selling monoclonal antibodies as research reagents and had begun work on diagnostic kits

2. Steve Shirley pictured in May 1981 on the roof of F International's headquarters in Chesham. Shortly afterwards the company moved to its present offices in nearby Berkhamsted

3. Mike Bevan, founder of Xionics, explains to the author the idea of the 'data exchange' in July 1982. He was by then already grappling with the problem of how to finance the next stage of his company's expansion

4. Hermann Hauser of Acorn Computers pictured in October 1981. On the table in front of him is an 'Atom' computer. The best-selling BBC computer would be launched early the following year

5. Peter Michael (front), Bob Graves (middle) and David Moulds (right) following a United Engineering Industries board meeting in Newbury in the autumn of 1983. Keith Duckworth, the fourth board member, was absent

6. Joe Franks of Ion Tech pictured in front of a large 'source' in the Teddington factory in the summer of 1983

7. Tom Melling and colleagues watch a model of an airship manoeuvring underwater at the Structural Dynamics HQ in Southampton. The date is September 1980. Melling, with moustache, is seen through a model of the Claymore oil production platform. He had just won the contract that was to kill Structural Dynamics, for the salvage of the *Alexander Kielland*.

their sponsor agreed to a 20 per cent price increase before the final launch in February. A number of retailing chains had expressed interest in the BBC micro, but had been told that they would have to make do with zero margins for the time being. Although the market would probably bear a further price increase quite easily, on both the Model 'A' and the more powerful Model 'B' machines, Acorn alone is not free to impose one. Pricing is in the hands of the BBC who have other considerations in mind apart from the profitability of their joint venture partner.

The BBC computer, with its extraordinary expandability, will be the centrepiece of Acorn's product development strategy over the next five years or so.

Already spin-off products have appeared and more are in the pipeline. There is a cheaper version called the 'Electron' aimed at the hobby/home market and a number of more expensive machines including the £600 'Gluon' add-on aimed at small business users and, in a networked configuration, aimed at larger companies too. There is also a new stand-alone product called the 'Omega' which incorporates the 'Gluon 2'. This add-on is powered by National Semiconductor's advanced 32-bit processor, the 16032.

Floppy disc drives, printers and monitors have all come or are coming on stream. The software library is being built up rapidly. Acorn is unusual at this end of the market in having a substantial 'in-house' applications software facility in the shape of its Acornsoft subsidiary. Other companies rely on outside software houses to generate a new machine's software library.

Acorn does not mind if other people write software for its computers and, if it did mind, there is little it could do about it. But Hauser and Curry believe the presence of Acornsoft helps to maintain the standards of software produced by outsiders. In the end it is largely the quality of the software which decides whether a computer succeeds or fails in the business market.

Hauser and Curry are beginning to feel strong enough now to think about taking on the American big boys like Commodore, Apple, Sirius, Tandy, DEC, Data General and the mighty IBM, not to mention the emerging Japanese companies like Sord. All of these rivals are bulging with marketing muscle but all of them have one serious disadvantage – they are attacking the business micro market from the top downwards. Hauser and Curry are convinced that there are substantial strategic advantages in attacking the market from the bottom. That is, after all, the direction in which evolution works.

Apart from the insight the Acorn story gives into the opportunities at the 'interface' between the academic and business worlds, it sheds light on another quality of the modern, high-technology company. Acorn has long grown past the stage where the conventional wisdom would have expected it to set up a production facility, and yet the company still has no wish to engage in manufacturing.

Hauser and Curry take the view that they do not need to get involved in manufacturing – that what Acorn is good at, research, design, development and marketing, is quite sufficient to build a healthy business on.

The example of Clive Sinclair's ill-fated venture into manufacturing at St Ives is fresh in Curry's memory particularly. It has also convinced Sinclair himself of the folly of manufacturing. Hauser says that if you have a manufacturing facility and it encounters difficulties, you are obliged to spend time and effort on putting it right. If your sub-contractor fouls up, on the other hand, you just get another sub-contractor.

The corollary of this 'unbundling' of functions that have traditionally been carried out within one organisation is that in parallel with the development of design and marketing companies, there will emerge a new breed of specialist sub-contracting companies.

It seems probable that this new kind of stratification in industry will lead over the next decade or so to a clear division between ideas-based companies and production-based companies. They will work in partnership with each other but they will no longer belong to each other. One could say that companies like Acorn are examples of 'neoteny' in action – they are deliberately holding the non-manufacturing quality of youthful companies into their early maturity.

If this is the way forward for Western business (it does not look as if it is for Japanese business), then the fact that Britain's design houses and consultancies are widely admired throughout the world is one reason to be hopeful about our economic prospects.

7

Peter Michael, Bob Graves and Micro Consultants

There was, in Peter Michael's view, a certain inevitability about his gravitation towards the business life. He was born in Purley on 17 June 1938, into a family where the creeds and conventions of commerce, and the trappings of successful enterprise, were all in evidence.

Unlike others he did not rebel against the business world and try to shape his life around its antithesis; he liked it. He enjoyed the travelling, the socialising and the overall ambience of a business family. But perhaps to his father's regret, Peter Michael was never very interested in stamps. After the war Mick Michael opened a philately shop next door to Stanley Gibbons in The Strand, London. In the fullness of time the two operations merged and Mick Michael ended up as chairman of the Stanley Gibbons group. Despite his philatelic blind spot, young Peter was bright and business-minded, with a good head for figures and a fondness for machinery of all kinds. He started his first business while at the Whitgift School in Croydon where he shone in mathematics and physics. He won a place at London University's Queen Mary College to read electronics.

Between school and QMC he took a year off to work in industry, with the Muirhead facsimile company. While there he filed his first patent application for a device called a 'double balance modulator using junction diodes'. He remembers going to the US embassy (it was a US patent he had applied for) and receiving the token silver dollar then given to all successful patent applicants.

Michael went up to QMC in 1958. 'I wasn't a brilliant student', he calls, 'but I do remember finding the physics interesting.' He preferred the application of theory to theorising; he liked being able to do things with the technology. The young engineer worked during the vacations with Rolls-Royce on vibration – a subject the aero-engine giant was becoming increasingly interested in as the development of its fateful RB211 engine progressed. (See chapter 9.)

He also had time to get quite deeply involved in motor cars, his fondness for which remains. He built two Ford 'specials' while at QMC. Exotic glass-fibre bodies were available then, before tax changes knocked the bottom out of the kit car market, which the enterprising hobbyist would attach to the chassis of an old saloon car.

Peter was the proud owner for a while of a two-seater, R4 Jowett Jupiter which he still believes was an under-rated and very under-developed motor car. He was one of those thousands of youngsters who were on the edge of motor sport; intensely interested in everything that was going on, but never really participating. His friend and collaborator Bob Graves, on the other hand, was in the thick of it. He raced 500cc Formula 3 cars and was a genuine ace on two-wheels – he still holds a lap record for motorbikes at Silverstone, achieved on a 350cc, single-cylinder KTT Velocette. He will hold the record in perpetuity because they changed the circuit soon afterwards.

After graduating from QMC in 1961, Michael joined Smiths Industries as an instrumentation engineer. He was full of enthusiasm. 'I left university with a strange idea,' he recalls. 'I thought that work was all that mattered. Boy! Was I going to show them what it was all about.'

He was posted to the KLG spark-plug test house at Putney Vale, London, where there was an interesting collection of engines, including a single-cylinder generator that happened to be proving a pig to start on the day Michael arrived. He was asked to see if he could get it going, so he rolled up his sleeves and began to strip the engine down. It was like rubbing Aladdin's lamp. He had just got elbow-deep in oil and grease when a shop steward appeared as if by magic. Michael was an instrumentation engineer and instrumentation engineers were not supposed to get their hands dirty. That was the fitter's job.

'Where's your card, lad?' the steward demanded, and when Peter failed to produce evidence of union membership, he was rewarded with a front row seat at a real, live industrial dispute.

The shop steward called a strike and the fitters walked out.

'I realised then', Peter Michael recalls, 'that work was not just about work.'

Despite this inauspicious start, he enjoyed his three years at Smiths Industries. He got married while he was there and moved around, with stints at and visits to practically all of the company's plants from Cricklewood to Chatham.

But by 1964 Peter was becoming conscious of a strong desire to get more intimately involved with pure electronics. When he worked for Muirhead he had been dealing with thermionic valves. By the time he was doing his holiday jobs for Rolls-Royce as an undergraduate, commuting from London to Derby in his home-made Ford specials, transistors were beginning to make their appearance. It was clear that electronics technology was advancing rapidly and Peter Michael wanted to get more intimately involved with that advance.

So he left Smiths and joined Plessey. The electronics company had just begun a detailed search for automation possibilities and Peter Michael's first posting was as a member of that search team.

Looking back he believes he was extremely fortunate throughout his early career in industry in that coincidentally all the jobs he was given required him to meet and talk with the key people in the companies concerned. 'I realised', he remarked, 'that the companies were run by no more than half-a-dozen key people, here and there – all the others were just hanging on. Because of my jobs, I got to know them all.'

Peter Michael's whistle-stop automation tour round Plessey convinced him that the most interesting part of the group was the work John Maddison and his team were doing on thin-film hybrid circuits. 'I manoeuvred myself so that I was working for Maddison', Peter recalls. 'He had just set up the thin-film hybrid circuit facility and there were some very interesting people working there.' The project was part of Plessey's special purpose machines division and one of Peter Michael's tasks there was to develop a way of formalising the specifications of different machines to make it easier to draw up circuit diagrams. 'I was always interested,' he says, 'in the interface between electronics and the machine.'

Peter Michael always knew that he would go independent some time. In 1967 he felt ready. His general interests and aptitudes had emerged at school; his practical approach to electronics began first to develop in Bob Graves's TV repair workshop; an awareness of his own innovative qualities dawned during his time with Muirhead and Rolls-Royce; his interest in business, given free rein at home, was strengthened by his friendship with Graves.

There was a time at Plessey when he toyed with the idea of embarking on a more intellectual career, but in retrospect this could be seen as merely a tidying up exercise.

The process is revealed in the subjects Peter Michael chose to study in his spare time. He began with post-graduate work in nuclear physics and then progressed to the slightly more practical subject of aeronautics. Then he became bored with three-dimensional, differential equations and decided to learn a little about management.

He signed up with the British Institute of Management for a three-year, three-evenings-a-week diploma course in management studies. He says, 'I thought management might be easier.' In retrospect Michael does not believe he benefited enormously from the BIM course. 'I learned an awful lot about budgetary control,' he says, 'but you learn more about management from running your own company for six weeks than from three years of formal training.'

By far the most impressive teacher encountered on the BIM course was the redoubtable Vic Feather of the TUC, later Lord Feather, who was a visiting lecturer. Michael says that if he had met Feather earlier he would never have made that terrible industrial relations gaffe at the KLG test house on the day he joined Smiths Industries.

But though Peter Michael believes there is no substitute for direct experience of running a business, the fact that he signed up for the BIM course and completed his three years, indicates his mind-set at the time. He was clearly beginning to see his career in terms of management. He felt he needed a good grounding in the subject though he was probably not clear in his own mind at the time about the use he would put the knowledge to.

Another key element in the timing of the decision was that Michael had spotted a market opportunity. As we have seen, his interests were focussed on the electronics/machine interface – that threshold between the information processing electronic circuits and the machines they were designed to control.

It seemed obvious to Michael in 1967 that the advent of the digital computer was going to change things. It works much faster than the 'analogue' computer and if full advantage was to be made of the extra speed a great deal of work needed to be done with all kinds of electronically-controlled devices to enable them to understand the new digital *lingua franca*.

Michael believed Plessey should begin to prepare for the digital revolution and he said as much. Higher up the company they were not convinced, so Peter Michael decided to do it himself. 'I hoped I'd earn a crust,' he says of his decision to go independent, 'but the real motivation was to be able to do some of the things I wanted to do and to do them properly.' So he had the inclination – 'I was 29 by then,' he says, 'I'd been in industry for six years. I thought I knew a thing or two' – he had the market opportunity, he had a very supportive wife, but he knew next to nothing about selling.

Bob Graves did though. Graves was educated by the same foundation as Peter Michael but for financial reasons he never made it to university. He does not think he was really the university type. He preferred to pick up his education in less formal ways, like playing truant from school at the age of 15 to take and pass his exam for a radio transmitting licence (he had been running a pirate transmitting station for two years by then) and devouring vast amounts of information from technical journals of all kinds.

He had a brief spell in a drawing office before joining the RAF to do his national service. On demobilisation he got a job as a radio and TV engineer at a time when independent television was just starting. The leading TV manufacturers were producing special converters to permit reception of the new channel on old sets, but in the vicinity of Crystal Palace, where Bob Graves was working, the converters were practically useless, 'Unless', Graves recalls, 'you enjoyed watching two programmes simultaneously!' Graves and a fellow employee were appalled not only by the inefficiency of the devices but also by their size. They decided to develop their own converter. Graves says, 'It was a fraction of the size of anything else and it worked like a dream.'

He and his collaborator decided to leave their jobs and set up a small manufacturing facility. They made and fitted hundreds of their converters and earned enough money to buy out an established hi-fi and TV business in Addiscombe. They continued their manufacturing activities alongside the retail business and made many hundreds more converters which they sold in kit form under the name C&G Kits.

They hired, on a part-time basis, a youngster called Tony Valentine (now better known as the actor Anthony Valentine). One morning he failed to show, having rushed off to an audition. Another young lad arrived and announced that he had come instead of Tony and what did they want him to do first? The answer was 'Move your ***** bicycle from cluttering up the entrance.' Thus Bob Graves met Peter Michael.

Young Peter turned out to be an industrious, diligent and strikingly gifted helper for Graves and his partner. The part-time employee/employer relationship lasted, with the odd gap for Muirhead and Rolls-Royce, right through to the time Michael joined Smiths.

Graves remembers particularly the occasion Michael first exhibited his prodigious inventive powers. It was during Peter's time at QMC. A well-known wireless magazine had published an article about a solid-state diode which, for some curious reason, changed its capacitance relative to an applied voltage. For most readers it was simply a strange phenomenon – for Peter Michael it was a clear case of a solution in search of a problem. Within a month Michael had found such a problem: the control of an FM (Frequency Modulated) radio signal. He incorporated the discovery into Britain's first push-button, AFC (Automatic Frequency Control), FM radio. His timing was perfect. The BBC had just installed its first VHF (Very High Frequency) transmission station at Wrotham Hill, in Kent.

They marketed the tuner in kit form for £7-19s-6d a time and it sold in hundreds. The only problem, and it fell to Bob Graves to sort it out, was that Michael, in his enthusiasm, had sold the exclusive design to two competing radio magazines.

In 1964 Bob's partner became seriously ill with a form of leukaemia and it was decided to sell the business, which was by then turning over about £100,000 a year, to Robinson Rentals. Graves took a year's sabbatical on his share of the proceeds and became involved with the publishing industry. At the time his brother George was a successful journalist turned public relations man.

The brothers helped a certain John Smith to found the weekly motoring newspaper *Motoring News*. Bob was the technical writer and was in charge of road testing. The paper was too successful. Circulation soared and it got to the point when demand was so great that they were unable to pay for the print run which had to be settled in advance. Looking back, Bob Graves believes it was a mistake to have gone weekly straight away – it was just too much to do on a part-time basis. *Motoring News* was later sold to *Motorsport* and still flourishes.

Graves was undecided about what to do next. Through his journalistic contacts he drifted into the IPC publishing group where he worked for a while on *Motor* before moving to *Motorship*. But it was always going to be just an episode. He did not like working for other people. 'I was deciding which way to jump,' he says of his eighteen months with IPC.

(The time was not wasted. The experience was exploited later when Bob and Peter agreed to start an electronics journal in partnership with two names from Bob's interlude with publishing, Bill Gledhill and Mike Brown. *Systems International* became a leading publication in its field and was ultimately sold to Bob's old employer, IPC, for some £400,000. The four-way partnership continues with a business magazine, *Mind Your Own Business*.)

Meantime Graves was seeing quite a bit of Peter Michael. 'Peter was despondent,' Graves recalls. 'I had several sessions with him trying to cheer him up.' Michael had acquired by then his interest in interface devices for digital computers and was becoming increasingly frustrated by his employer Plessey's refusal to get into the area.

So Graves and Michael decided to form Micro Consultants.

'We were very complementary characters,' says Bob Graves.

'Pete had enormous ambition and drive and outstanding technical ability. But he was impatient with detail, and his experience didn't always match up with his aspirations.' Graves says Michael's style was indigestible for some; he acquired the reputation in certain quarters of being a bit of a line-shooter. 'But I knew it wasn't just talk,' says Graves. 'He has a great ability to rationalise problems. I had had experience of his inventiveness and of his capacity for hard work.'

Graves believes that what he brought to the partnership was a broad technical grounding, an ability to influence people and a wide circle of mature and well-qualified friends. Michael described the Graves contribution more succinctly: 'He is a wise man.'

In Bob Graves's view, friends are essential for those starting up new businesses. You need to get help in all sorts of areas at the start, before you can afford to pay for it. A friendly bank manager is also a great asset. Peter Michael found one at the Midland Bank branch near his home in Billericay. The manager listened with interest to the Michael/Graves business plan and responded positively to Michael's request for overdraft facilities if and when they might be needed. Indeed, the manager offered borrowing facilities considerably in excess of what the entrepreneurs had expected on the basis of the limited collateral they had available. Such enlightened branch banking has its reward. The company has stayed with the same branch ever since.

The original idea was that the new business should be mostly consultancy jobs supported by a few products. In the event it turned out to be mostly products supported by a few consultancy jobs. 'I don't know about Pete,' says Graves, 'but I certainly didn't think we'd grow into a multi-million pound company in a few years.'

They set up shop in Graves's own small work-room at his home in Coulsdon, Surrey. They had a few thousand pounds between them and the plan was first to spend some time developing Michael's digital interfacer ideas. After five months of extremely hard work, during which both men were living electronics in their waking and dreaming hours, it was time for Bob Graves to go out and start knocking on doors. They soon found that although there was plenty of work around, it was terribly difficult to persuade large companies to hire a young consultancy firm with no track record.

In the event this turned out to be a blessing in disguise. One particular large company had just won a contract for the development of a new missile system and was finding it very hard to get a device known as a Digital to Analogue converter, which translates the output of a computer into the more familiar rising and falling voltage code (analogue), to meet specification.

The device needed to convert one million instructions a second to within an accuracy of 0.5 per cent, it had to work over a wide range of temperatures and it had to be no larger than a pack of 10 cigarettes. The state of the art at the time could only provide a converter capable of translating 10,000 instructions a second. Even then it would measure a much too bulky 19 × 3 × 14 inches.

The company concerned responded to the MC approach by saying: 'You're not sufficiently well-established for us to give you a design and development contract, but you have the problem; if you can solve it, we'll buy the device from you in large numbers.'

It was not an ideal proposition because it meant that no money would be coming in unless or until Graves and Michael cracked the problem. It was all there was in the way of business, however, and it was a well-defined problem of the kind the new company had been preparing to confront. The two men, working alone mostly but with the help of a few friends, designed and tested a device that performed to specifications within six weeks. That a small company, barely six months old, should have been capable of solving a problem that was beyond the abilities of all the major groups active in the field should be more inspiring than surprising.

As Peter Michael had already discovered, no matter how large and well-staffed a corporate research and development department is, its creativity depends in the ultimate analysis on the skill and inventive vision of a few people. Had Michael stayed with Plessey he would undoubtedly have become a member of such an elite. As it was his abilities bore fruit in his own company. He was one of the few people in the country at the time who understood the potential of the new solid-state electronic devices that were becoming available; he was one of an even smaller group of engineers capable of dreaming up uses for the devices that even their inventors had failed to spot; he was probably unique in having spent five months of intense exploratory effort in the specific area of digital interfacing.

The D-A converter was a huge success. It provided the financial launch-pad for Micro Consultants, enabling the company to grow rapidly and to establish itself as a world leader in its field within just a few years. This was due in large part to the failure of Graves to make that first project a straightforward consultancy contract. If he had succeeded, the rights to the converter would have belonged to the client company. MC would have earned a fee and that would have been that as far as the converter's revenue potential was concerned. In the event, the rights to the design remained with MC and Graves made the most of them.

That single product generated £100,000 of revenue in the first two years. MC only finally stopped making it in 1981. 'We made hundreds of them', Graves remarked. 'Everything else grew out of that. We were lucky not to have given away our brains.'

Looking back Graves identified two principles which he believes stood the company in good stead during the early years. The first was MC's tidy-minded approach to electronic engineering. Peter Michael is an engineer's engineer. Not only could he devise circuits and component configurations that would do clever things; he also produced devices that were neatly made and elegantly designed. This was important in a market where the customer is usually an engineer too.

Secondly, the one area in which the young company never stinted itself was in the quality and quantity of instruments and tools with which the workshop was equipped. Both Graves and Michael, who in the course of building up their business saw the inside of a large number of R&D laboratories, were frequently appalled by the shortage of equipment and even more by its quality. They saw the effect this had on the people working in those places. Graves believes that this feature in many UK labs was alone responsible for a significant part of the notorious 'brain drain' that was taking place in the late 1960s and which seriously sapped British industry's ability to take up the challenges of the new technologies as they appeared.

For the rest, Graves puts down the D-A converter achievement to the passions and enthusiasms of the two men and to their enormous capacity for hard and sustained work. Such application is rarely found in large companies; sometimes it is the only way to make the technical breakthrough.

And it is important, in the view of Bob Graves, that this energy and industriousness should be maintained as the company begins to prosper. 'That's how you fuel the business,' he says. 'It's no good if the directors start buying new houses and larger cars and begin taking time off for a round of golf.'

The D-A converter spawned a family of similar products, including its obvious corollary, an A-D converter. Then people started coming to MC for consultancy and design work. Some contracts were accepted, but the lesson had been learned. There is more money to be made out of products than out of service. Thenceforth they were always looking for new products and when they found one, it became the stepping stone to another.

But as always, success brings with it new problems. A reputation for excellence in a particular area attracts predators. Graves remembers one occasion when an MC device had been lent to a large company for assessment. It failed to elicit the expected order and instead the same company brought out a carbon copy of the gadget a few months later. 'We were very disillusioned,' he recalls, 'but at that stage we couldn't afford to patent everything. It wasn't practical when big companies were involved.' This blatant piece of plagiarism did have one effect. Thereafter the company developed the habit of removing identification marks on some components and encapsulating others. That made plagiarism more difficult.

MC began laying long-term plans as the converter market expanded but Graves stresses they were never hard and fast. He says plans are important because 'you've got to give yourself direction' but equally important, in his view, is a readiness to alter plans and if necessary abandon them altogether in the light of events.

A case in point is the affair of MC's digital mini-computer. Having developed, with the help of computers, a product line of devices for use with computers, it was not long before MC was designing complete systems of which a computer made by someone else was a component. At that time the mini-computer market was experiencing a period of explosive growth, and hardware was in very short supply. Customers were having to wait a year or more for delivery and when the hardware finally arrived it cost a fortune.

When a computer scientist came to Graves and Michael with a design for a digital mini-computer that seemed ideal for the scientific market, they thought they had found a way of overcoming these problems. They bought the design, spent some time developing it and then went into production. The machine was called the 1601. It was well received in the marketplace and was comfortably profitable. MC made 100 of them and then stopped. The original plan had been for a run of 200, but Graves and Michael thought about it and decided to take their profit half-way through.

The decision was an important one. The scientific computer market was and is huge. Though dominated then by IBM, it was already becoming apparent that 'Big Blue' could be profitably challenged by smaller companies like Control Data and DEC. The temptation to go ahead with computers was thus real enough, especially with one successful product already under the MC belt. Computers were, after all, the biggest game in town and entrepreneurs relish playing David to industrial Goliaths.

But Graves and Michael also knew that the computer industry was changing fast and that large sums of money would be needed to develop second- and third-generation machines. They decided that theirs was not that sort of company. They had no enthusiasm for building up the mass production skills and facilities that would be needed to enter the market on a long-term basis.

They had the brainpower to do it, but not the finance or, as it turned out, the inclination. They decided that they liked life at the sharp end of technology too much to step back from the frontiers of technological change and involve themselves in mass production. Who knows, had the decision gone the other way they might have ridden the mini-boom in the 1970s and then the micro-boom in the 1980s!

But the company would have been forced to change. It would have had a long-term commitment and thus much narrower horizons. One of its strengths has been its flexibility – its willingness to give its technical staff their heads in the knowledge that mistakes will inevitably be made.

MC advertises for staff now alongside all the other large electronics groups but in those days the brainpower on which its success has been based was accumulated in a very personal way. It comes back to the importance Graves attaches to friends: 'You hire Jack because you know he's a red hot engineer and you hope that when the time comes Jack will recommend Jim who's equally hot in another area. That's the way you build up teams when you're small.'

The story of Micro Consultants from 1967 to the present is one of rapid and remarkably steady growth. There was one serious crisis though, which might have proved fatal. It happened towards the end of 1971. Business was booming by then, but it became clear as Christmas approached that the company had overstretched itself. Graves and Michael looked at the projects on the go at the time and they realised that if just one of them went wrong they would have a serious problem on their hands – 'like going bust' is how Graves puts it.

It was simply a question of inadequate financial controls and they made sure it never happened again. Graves remembers the time all too well: 'There was a dizzy sort of feeling that it was all slipping away from us. We suddenly became aware of how easily things could get out of hand.' What changed afterwards was not that the company became less willing to take risks; it was that Graves and Michael realised the importance of being able to say 'no' and of the need to monitor the company's progress more closely.

Peter Michael admits he was wrong about the digital interfacer market. The sort of business he had in mind when he decided to leave Plessey and go into MC with Graves did not develop until nearly a decade later. But there was another market, which Peter Michael describes as 'more researchy, semi-military, higher precision', which fell into their laps. In retrospect this too can be regarded as a stroke of luck.

If the market had developed as quickly as Michael expected it to and on as broad a front, then the competition might have been stiffer at the beginning, before MC had built up its financial and marketing strengths. As it was, the digital interfacer market evolved slowly and remained of insufficient size for a number of years to attract the attention of the big boys.

That gave MC the breathing space it needed to gather its strength. By the time the large companies began to take the business seriously they found that during the intervening years a sizeable operation had grown up, which enjoyed an enviable reputation in scientific circles and which was literally years ahead in the technology.

The rate of change began to gather pace in the early 1970s. Michael and Graves, building on their success with converters, became interested in developing devices that worked fast. Since digital computers were attractive because of their speed, it was clearly desirable to attempt to emulate that speed as closely as possible in the converters. High-speed conversion techniques were therefore the leading edge – the targets, so to speak – of research and development. A number of companies were investigating what appeared to be the most promising ways forward.

Peter Michael, never one to take accepted wisdom for granted, began to investigate a likely technique which everyone else had dismissed because of one obvious deficiency. He studied it and came up with some modifications which completely avoided the problem his rivals had deemed fatal.

'We made some very high-speed converters,' Bob Graves recalls, 'but there was no obvious market for them. We began to look around for applications.'

Graves says this episode illustrates one of the two development paths the MC group has pursued. One is fuelled by customers; they come along to the company with a problem and MC solves it. The other is fuelled by Peter Michael's curiosity more than anything else and by the conviction that in high-technology industries every pound spend on general research and development is well spent.

Both approaches have proved fruitful. Bob Graves reckons that the group's development has been inspired equally by both types of stimulus. Customer-led problem-solving has alternated with the more general technological breakthrough; the former has paced out the steps along a trail blazed by the latter.

They found a market for their very high-speed converter. Once again, it was a researchy, semi-military sort of application in the radar field. This brought Graves and Michael into contact with the cathode ray tube, the basis of the television receiver, and it also confronted them with demands for even more speed.

Their radar customers pressed them so much that before long MC was producing devices capable of 'digitising' a complete monochrome TV picture. The incentive then was obvious – to increase the speed to the point when they could digitise an entire colour TV picture.

Once that was done, MC was emerging from that profitable but still relatively small 'researchy' end of the market and was poised on the brink of something very much more substantial. It was not long before the word got out that it was now possible to digitise an entire TV picture. To the initiated this was clearly a major development and there was one immediately obvious application.

Until the time Graves and Michael formed their Quantel subsidiary to service the TV market, video recorders were something of a luxury in the TV industry. The technology in use was terribly convenient but it was difficult to get just right. Everything had to be ultra-high precision and video recorders suitable for broadcasting were thus very expensive. They came mostly from the US companies RCA and Ampex and they cost anything up to £100,000 apiece. The Japanese were making much cheaper, £10,000 machines, but the picture stability was simply not good enough for broadcasting.

And then along came Quantel with a device that could encode and store two lines of a TV picture. This made it possible for a video picture to be captured on a £10,000 recorder, stored in Quantel's black box and then spewed out again with all the imperfections ironed out. The device was called a 'digital time base correcter' and overnight it reduced the cost of video hardware by an order of magnitude.

The product boomed for a couple of years before a number of other manufacturers assimilated the principle and precipitated the inevitable downward price spiral. However, the highly profitable years of Quantel's virtual monopoly had been used to develop the world's first portable, digital synchroniser, that could store a complete frame of a TV picture. By the time the newly emerging digital video industry had caught up with that,

Quantel had moved on once more and produced the world's first, practical video effects machine.

The time bought and the money generated by this string of pioneering achievements has enabled Quantel to develop a whole range of digital TV products and to establish itself as the unchallenged world leader in the field.

In 1981 Quantel won a Montreux Achievement Gold Medal for its range of digital processing equipment for broadcast TV. Its parent company, Micro Consultants, sports two Queen's Awards for technical achievement and an Emmy Award from the National Academy of Television Arts and Sciences. And for Quantel's dynamic managing director Richard Taylor there was an OBE.

The glittering prizes that have been showered on the Micro Consultants group over the years all boil down to technological lead. Quantel's digital framestore product line defines what the state-of-the-art is in broadcast TV.

The intriguing part of it all from Quantel's point of view is that the digitalisation of TV has really only just begun. The TV industry worldwide is now locked in a spasm of frantic computerisation that is likely to continue unabated for a decade or more. Not only does this provide the company with substantial, long-term growth potential; it also provides the MC group with an enviable recession-proof quality for, as luck would have it, the TV industry into which MC fell almost by accident tends to boom when the rest of the economy is ailing.

It is not hard to imagine how MC might have developed somewhat differently. It could have embraced the computer business with more enthusiasm and, if its efforts had met with success, it could have 'matured' into a mass-production company. That is, after all, the conventional development route for high technology companies, according to the conventional wisdom at any rate.

An innovative company is supposed to use the time and money generated by its technological lead to invest in larger production facilities so that it can 'expose' its technological edge to as large a market as possible. According to this view the technological lead begins by providing a temporary monopoly and ends up as merely a price advantage in a competitive market.

MC deliberately rejected this route when it decided to pull out of computer manufacturing. Graves and Michael decided to use their technological lead to finance the development of new products rather than the larger-scale production of existing ones. Developing the principle applied in the computer decision, they might have rejected the digital TV opportunity when it appeared, arguing that it was, like computers, a much larger market demanding a heavy investment in selling and carrying the risk that a host of powerful competitors might appear at any moment.

So far the flexible strategy applied by Graves and Michael seems to have paid off. The emphasis on products rather than services, which was more by accident than design at the start, has not yet forced them to become involved in costly and hazardous mass manufacturing.

The scale of production has increased but so has the size of the company. What might have been risky five years ago is less so now.

A couple of years ago a major threat to the company appeared in the form of a lawsuit alleging patent infringement, mounted in the US by a major, international electronics company. The US commercial courts are littered with the corpses of young companies whose time, money and energy have been taken up in prolonged lawsuits, kept going for years with interrogatories, injunctions and the like by more powerful competitors. Had the challenge come earlier and had it been more skilfully mounted, MC might have joined those slaughtered corporate innocents. As it was the company was rich enough to buy the best legal advice and was confident enough to go on the attack. MC took the device they were accused of having copied to pieces, found that it was in fact a direct copy of one of their own and promptly launched a countersuit. It soon became clear that MC's case was considerably stronger than that of the original litigant and the matter was quickly settled out of court to the British company's advantage.

MC patents much more than it used to but does not rely too much on patent protection; as Bob Graves explained, 'No patent means anything until it has been tested in the courts.' In his view a more fruitful approach to maintaining equity in one's ideas is to pursue an active cross-licensing policy designed to recruit powerful licensee friends to one's cause in the event of a legal challenge.

As we have seen, friends loom large in the Graves view of business. They are, in a way, substitutes for the sheer size that is normally taken to be essential for survival in the big business jungle.

The acquisition by United Engineering Industries of the MC group in the closing weeks of 1981 was no ordinary takeover. For one thing MC was comparable in size and even more so in growth potential to the whole of UEI. Indeed, so large was MC in relation to its bidder that some observers characterised the deal as a 'reverse takeover'.

But this missed the point. The UEI/MC merger had very little to do with the collection of motivations normally associated with corporate get-togethers. It was not inspired by a feeling of vulnerability on the part of either party; there was no evidence of the 'if you can't beat them, buy them' principle having been at work; there was little informed talk of industrial 'synergy' and there has never been, during or since the merger, any mention of 'rationalisation'.

In a way the UEI group looks a bit like a return to the now generally discredited idea of the industrial conglomerate that was briefly fashionable in the late 1960s and early 1970s, but it is not like that either. Little attempt has been made to knit together common functions like management accounting, research and development or buying and selling. The group members retain all the autonomy they enjoyed before joining UEI.

So why is Bob Graves irritated when people suggest that UEI is no more than the sum of its parts? If no attempts are being made to knit the organisation together as would ordinarily be the case, why should anyone expect the company as a whole to perform better than its individual parts would have performed independently? Part of the reason, according to Graves, is that the merger has widened the circle of his and Peter's friends. They now enjoy quite an intimate relationship with a number of successful entrepreneurs operating in high technology industries. Though they are co-operators rather than competitors, they speak the same language. There is a great deal of mutual respect and because of that Graves and Michael are finding there is quite a bit of cross-fertilisation of ideas.

One can imagine an informal discussion between Peter Michael and fellow UEI 'club' member Keith Duckworth, following a UEI board meeting. Duckworth is the technical genius behind the Cosworth V8, the most successful Formula One racing engine of all time, but he is aware that turbocharged engines from the continent have begun to threaten its dominance.

He is faced with a straightforward problem of commercial strategy: should he develop his own turbocharged engine now or should he wait to see what emerges from a review of the current formula in 1984? Peter Michael, though he has retained his interest in motor racing, has earned his entrepreneurial spurs in quite a different area. He can bring a fresh eye to Duckworth's dilemma and perhaps suggest strategies that Duckworth has overlooked. At the same time Duckworth will feel strengthened by the association with his fellow UEI members. It may be that his best strategy is to throw himself into the business of lobbying for a change in the formula that favours him, just as rivals like Renault, Ferrari and BMW are doing. If that is the case, Duckworth will feel more sanguine about his chances with the combined weight of UEI behind him than he would have done had Cosworth remained independent.

Bob Graves talks of having found 'a second wind' following the UEI merger and he points to another, less obvious advantage. He says that as entrepreneurs grow older they begin to worry about who will succeed them. He and Michael have identified likely successors within MC but until the merger with UEI there was no way to give them 'hands-on', top-management experience without retiring themselves.

Now, under the UEI umbrella, there is room for them to move 'upstairs' so to speak, as more-or-less full-time members of the UEI board, and still be able to keep a close watch on how their protégés shape up at Micro Consultants. What UEI hopes to demonstrate is that the things that are left undone during the consummation of a merger are as important as the things that are done. If most mergers are like marriages, then membership of the UEI group is much more like belonging to a club.

It remains to be seen whether the UEI experiment will go the way of the earlier conglomerates, or whether it really does represent a new, looser, more durable form of corporate association that has set a pattern others will follow. I incline to the latter prognosis. It seems to me that this new, federal form of association is an outgrowth of the Graves 'friends' theory of small business. It looks like an example of neoteny at work.

8
Dr Joe Franks and Ion Tech

One of the problems with high technology is that often it is so 'high' that for the layman it is simply out of sight.

In Britain the capital markets are staffed and run mainly by laymen. There is a great deal of excellent British technology that goes to waste simply because those whose function it is to finance such ventures do not know enough about the technologies concerned. The story of Dr Joe Franks and Ion Tech illustrates the problem. In this case, adequate and timely financing was forthcoming – had it not been, there would have been no story.

Dr Franks believes there are many inventions with commercial potential made in university, government and industrial research laboratories that never see the light of the market because of 'lack of insight, enthusiasm and funding at the right time'. Indeed, he suggests that the product his company was based on could have, theoretically, been developed half-a-century ago. Franks subscribes fully to the widely held view that Britain is strong in the first, inventive stage of new product development but is very weak compared particularly to Japan, in the second, production engineering stage.

Joe Franks was born on 26 March 1924 in Streatham, London. He had a conventional education, ending up in a grammar school at Bangor, North Wales, where he obtained 'A' levels in pure mathematics, applied maths and physics. He played tennis and squash – he was not much of a team game person – and he amused himself with the hobby of electronics. He went on to read physics at University College, London and then moved from there to Birkbeck College for his MSc, working part-time as a research assistant. He obtained his PhD in 1952. The subject of his thesis was the penetration of electrons into luminescent materials.

The natural next step would have appeared to be post-doctoral research, but Joe Franks has a very practical turn of mind. He is more interested in what can be done with technology than he is in the technology itself. So in 1952 he joined AEI's laboratories, working, amongst other things, on the growth of crystals, especially silicon crystals which were then in the process of becoming the basic materials of the semiconductor industry.

Franks ended up as section leader at the AEI labs in charge of the phosphors and photo conductor department, developing techniques to be used in optical detectors and emitters.

In 1963, as rumblings about a massive re-organisation of Britain's electrical and electronics industry began to grow in strength, he decided it was time for a change. He joined the research laboratories of Standard Telephones and Cables (the UK end of the American multinational, ITT), as an assistant manager responsible for research into the properties of another important semiconducting material, gallium arsenide.

At the time it was still very much a laboratory technology; Franks, though very interested in the work, was always looking over the shoulders of those 'downstream' from the labs to see what practical use his work was being put to. He stayed at STC for five years, until 1968. Towards the end of his time there he began to get involved in discussions with a number of colleagues about how irritating it could be working for a large company. 'When you're working in a research laboratory', he explained, 'you have very little control over what happens – events shape you. You never know when you are going to be switched to another project. One discusses these things.'

In the end the STC discontents (there were about half-a-dozen of them including Franks himself) decided to leave STC and set up their own company, Electrotech. The business plan was to explore with more vigour than STC had been willing to permit the technology of 'evaporation' used in optics for the coating of lenses and in solid-state electronics for the deposition of conductive surfaces onto semiconductor substrates. Franks became a director of Electrotech and had a small equity stake. The company, still based in Wales because that was the nearest Development Area to London, still prospers and is a leader in its field.

But evaporation technology, though important, is just one of a number of technologies that comprise the production engineering side of the modern semiconductor industry. Joe Franks became interested in another.

A government laboratory had some years previously developed a novel technique for producing 'ions' (atoms that have become electrically charged because of an excess or deficiency of electrons) using a particular kind of electromagnetic containment called a 'saddle-field'. As is usual in such cases the invention was passed over to the National Research Development Corporation (NRDC) which then went about its statutory business of hawking the technology around likely companies in an attempt to get the idea exploited commercially.

A number of groups showed sufficient interest to build a few prototypes but all of them encountered problems. The saddle-field ion source, though clearly a good idea in principle, proved difficult to engineer into an efficient product. Interest faded and the saddle-field beat a doleful retreat back to the NRDC. The Conventional Wisdom of the Dominant Group, which the late C. H. Waddington so aptly christened with the acronym 'COWDUNG', had formally declared the saddle-field source as 'no more than an interesting laboratory phenomenon.'

But Joe Franks felt this judgment was premature. Ion sources or 'guns' are widely used in laboratories for a number of purposes. They are particularly useful for the etching of fine structures such as optical and X-ray gratings and today they show promise as a key element in the production of the next generation of highly complex silicon 'chips'. The saddle-field source had aroused interested in the first place because it was clear that if it could be made to work efficiently it would be a very competitive product. It worked at pressures significantly higher than those employed in conventional 'cold cathode' ion sources, which meant that it would not require such expensive vacuum pumps.

Franks began to play around with the device, making modifications here, adjustments there and generally tightening up the engineering. He got the thing to work properly and he suggested to his colleagues at Electrotech that the company should develop the modified device to the production stage.

The idea was not taken up and so in 1971, at the age of 47, Joe Franks parted company with Electrotech, picking up a few thousand pounds for his shares, and set up his own company, Ion Tech. Recalling the decision, Dr Franks said: 'No-one seemed interested but I was convinced. Ideas like that don't come along very often. I knew I'd fail but I also knew that if I didn't do it I would regret it for the rest of my life.'

He went to his bank manager and explained his plans. The man was quite sympathic and on the strength of his customer's credit-worthiness and scientific reputation he agreed to a £10,000 overdraft facility – enough to get a prototype source up and running.

Franks had a number of friends at the University of Wales Institute of Science and Technology and they let him borrow the facilities and equipment he needed. He knew the ion source market well so he was not going into it blind. Most of the experts acknowledged that there would be a ready market for a higher pressure ion source – all they disputed was the Franks insistence that saddle-field technology could deliver such a source.

For a man so new to the business of running a company, Dr Franks displayed in those early days a remarkable grasp of the commercial pitfalls and possibilities. He had to go to the NRDC to get a licence to manufacture the device because the NRDC held the patent on the invention. But instead of signing on the dotted line straight away, he decided he would try for an exclusive licence. The NRDC was not and is not in the habit of granting exclusives, but Franks knew that the saddle field had already done the rounds without attracting a bite, so it was worth a try.

He got his exclusive licence, patented his own modifications (and they were what made the source efficient) and only then did he start hawking his wares around the scientific marketplace. The selling effort began with the delivery by Franks of a scientific paper in 1972, in which he explained what he had achieved. A representative of a company that was to become an important competitor of Ion Tech was very interested, but by then it was too late. Even if the exclusivity of the NRDC licence could have been broken, the company would have come up against the equally important Franks patents.

Franks recruited an engineer to get his embryonic production line going and he went out selling. 'Having lived all my life until then in a laboratory,' he recalls, 'it gave me a completely different view of the world.' He cannot have made too bad a salesman because in what was left of 1972 he managed to sell ten saddle-field ion sources, complete with power supply, for £500 apiece. The first customer was the Post Office which used the device for etching semiconductor material. Franks says this early version was rudimentary by modern Ion Tech standards, but it did the job it was designed to do.

It soon emerged that Ion Tech's new sources could also be used for the 'thinning' of specimens to be studied under an electron microscope. Because electron microscopy employs an electron beam as a 'light' source, the specimens being studied need to be extremely thin. Ion beams are well suited for the role of the knife used to cut these infinitesimal slivers of material.

The idea of 'thinning' with ion sources first occurred to the French, but it caught on rapidly and a number of British and American companies were soon into the market. Ion thinning was thus established by the time Franks began to sell his saddle-field devices, so in addition to the conventional etching and cleaning applications, there was another ready-made market for his more efficient and more reliable machines. It was just a question of packaging the device differently, in the form of either an etching and cleaning kit or of a thinning kit.

In early 1973, less than two years after the establishment of Ion Tech, an opportunity for diversification presented itself. The same government laboratory from which the saddle-field source had first emerged, had been working over a period of some years, for its own purposes, on X-ray optics. It had developed a number of pioneering devices in an area which, in the early 1970s, was already beginning to show signs of substantial growth potential. Once again the NRDC was offered the technology and once again the NRDC began hawking it around the likely companies. This time, Ion Tech, which had impressed the laboratory and the NRDC with the skills it had displayed in the saddle-field development, was high on the list. After lengthy discussions it was agreed that the new X-ray optics technology should be transferred to Ion Tech. Franks packed up his Welsh company lock, stock and barrel, and established a new base at Teddington in South London.

It is hard to overestimate the degree of engineering excellence demanded of those working with X-ray optical components. When you are making devices designed to reflect radiation with a wave-length a thousand times shorter than that of light, you need to get the smoothness of your optical components exact to within a few Angstroms (an Angstrom Unit, named after the nineteenth century Swedish physicist Anders Angstrom, is equivalent to one ten billionth of a metre or one hundred-millionth of a centimetre).

Tolerances of this kind are not easy to achieve. Joe Franks says that in the realm of the Angstrom 'We are at the limit of what may be attained by present day engineering practice.' This is the main reason why Franks can say, with no immodesty, that 'We're the only X-ray optics people in the country.' He could have said, with equal justification, that 'We're the best X-ray optics people in the world.' As we shall see, Ion Tech's reputation in the X-ray optics field quickly became international.

But though the NRDC was clearly right to choose Ion Tech as the vehicle for the development, production and marketing of its client laboratory's work on X-ray optics, the high degree of engineering skills that had already distinguished the company was not, by itself, sufficient. Franks also needed money to get the new operation off the ground.

He approached the NRDC for financial help to transfer the technology into industry. There are well-defined provisions and criteria for such NRDC funding exercises, and the Ion Tech request qualified. Under such arrangements the NRDC lends money which the borrower repays on the basis of a previously agreed royalty on sales. When the original sum plus a charge for interest has been recouped, the royalty drops to a lower percentage for a period equal to the length of the original repayment schedule. It is in this second stage that the NRDC makes its profit.

Shortly after the Ion Tech X-ray optics division was established to produce flat and spherical X-ray reflecting mirrors, the company was asked to try its hand at making the X-ray telescopes for the UK6 satellite, later re-christened the Ariel 6. These telescopes employ paraboloid reflectors which are very much more difficult to make than the earlier flat or spherical mirrors. Ariel 6, which is still orbiting away out there, was a fine advertisement for Ion Tech technology.

The word was beginning to get around by then that the company was grappling successfully with what was generally regarded as extremely difficult engineering. In 1975, sub-contractors of America's National Aeronautics and Space Administration (NASA) approached Ion Tech and asked Franks and his colleagues if they could produce a paraboloid reflecting mirror in quartz for NASA's X-ray astronomy programme. The £27,000 contract was completed successfully and Ion Tech received a congratulatory telegram to honour the achievement.

The NASA sub-contractors, having failed to find a comparably competent company in the US, came back soon afterwards with another contract for the nickel-plating of a 50-centimetre-diameter X-ray telescope. Ion Tech had already been blooded in nickel-plating during the Ariel 6 contract when it had employed successfully a special plating process. In the case of the UK satellite, however, the mirrors had only been about 15 centimetres in diameter – the much larger NASA telescope presented problems of a different order. The nickel plate had to be capable of being highly polished so that it would reflect X-rays efficiently. American plating methods were simply not up to it, hence the approach to Ion Tech. Once again the contract was completed successfully.

During the following half-decade or so Ion Tech's reputation for ultra-high precision engineering, in the fields of both ion sources and X-ray optics, grew in stature and became widely known. New business was won all over the world, particularly in Japan, where buyers of technology are free from damaging prejudices such as 'not invented here' and its irksome cousin, especially evident in Britain, 'If the Americans haven't done it, then it can't be any good.'

When, in the summer of 1981, Ion Tech announced that it had developed the world's first compact beam 'atom source', known in the trade as the FAB (Fast Atom Bombardment) gas gun, Franks was inundated with inquiries, including phone calls from the mighty General Electric Corporation of the US and from such academic establishments as Harvard and the Massachusetts Institute of Technology.

But towards the end of the 1970s it was becoming apparent to Franks that the technology of X-ray telescopes and microscopes was about to enter a new phase, characterised by much larger and more expensive devices. A number of substantial companies such as Zeiss in Germany and Perkin Elmer in America were gearing themselves up for the market opportunities that lay ahead.

Ion Tech enjoyed a technological lead over the competition with the small stuff, but Franks could see the time approaching when this seedling market would disappear altogether. He felt he was faced with a choice; either stay with his current scale of operations and prepare to withdraw altogether from the X-ray optics market when it moved beyond his reach, devoting all his efforts to building up the ion gun side, or somehow find a way to take on the big boys.

Franks found the prospect of moving up in scale with the X-ray optics market very attractive. It looked as if X-ray microscopy might take-off dramatically in the mid-1980s and it was already clear that the 'big science' of particle physics, battling with fusion power and building ever larger testing facilities, was also veering more towards X-ray technology.

Franks was at the same time very conscious and not a little jealous of Ion Tech's lead. He did not want to give it up as the technology developed without a fight. He estimated that the entry fee into the big league would be about £1 million. Mindful perhaps of the reasoning that had launched him on his entrepreneurial career seven years earlier – 'I knew that if I didn't do it I'd regret it for the rest of my life' – he determined to make the attempt.

He approached his old friend NRDC and, simultaneously, he made contact with Midland Bank's venture-capital offshoot, Midland Bank Industrial Finance (MBIF). There followed a rather lengthy period of negotiation between the two prospective backers which Franks says, 'put us back a little'. That was a typically mild reproof to the NRDC, the MBIF and their respective teams of lawyers. In fact, time is of crucial importance for companies of this kind who compete not in terms of price but in terms of technological lead. It is especially important for a small company preparing to take on much larger groups, because the imbalance of marketing strength it will face can only be offset if the small company can get into the market well ahead of its rivals.

It was all sorted out in the end though. As part of the deal the X-ray Optics Division of Ion Tech was formed into a new company called Astron Developments and was moved out to spanking new factory facilities at the old Heston aerodrome. The operation is rattling around a bit there at the moment but if the market takes off as vigorously as Franks expects it to, Astron could be bursting at the seams within a few years.

In the event the NRDC ended up with 51 per cent of Astron, the MBIF got 11 per cent and Franks was left with 38 per cent. He does, however, retain an option to buy out the NRDC stake at any time he feels like it, if he can get the necessary funds together, so control of the new company is available if and when he wants it or can afford it. He says he didn't mind particularly surrendering voting control. He remains chairman and managing director of Astron and it is still, as far as he is concerned, very much his baby.

When I spoke to Dr Franks in the autumn of 1982, he was expecting the new venture to be breaking even by the end of that year. Franks believes that by 1990 both Astron and Ion Tech have a good chance of still being around. He would expect them to be about the same size by then, generating some £20 million worth of sales a year at current prices and earning an average of a 15 per cent return on sales. That is assuming that the X-ray optics market grows steadily rather than explodes as it might also do. In that event Astron would be considerably bigger by the end of the decade.

Both companies will probably have grown out of their present premises by then. Ion Tech, despite the space liberated by the departure of the X-ray optics division, will almost certainly have to move to a purpose-built factory within the next two years. Astron, still with ample spare space, will move later. Still looking towards 1990, Franks expects Ion Tech to be capable of serving the world market for its products from the factory it moves to next, whereas Astron may have had to move twice by the end of the decade.

The big unknown is the X-ray optics market. A large chunk of it depends on massive, government-funded projects like space telescopes, satellites and 'synchrotrons'. That makes the market vulnerable to the axe-wielding of spending-conscious governments.

Ion Tech's market, however, is beginning to move out of that phase. At the moment it is still based very much on electron-microscopy and deposition units used in universities and research establishments but it may not be for much longer.

The excellence of the company's products and the development of more heavy-duty versions of the ion and atom guns are opening up the industrial market. In the future, Ion Tech's performance will be more closely related to the level of activity in the semiconductor manufacturing industry which, despite the odd hiccup along the way, seems set for strong growth over the next decade.

Franks says he has got the production side sorted now and, with his new partners, he feels the finances of the two companies are sound. The next task is to get the marketing right. Selling overseas used to be done by agents supplied with exclusive rights to all products. Franks believes that was a mistake and the policy now is to grant agencies only for individual products. Franks says 'Agents work for the people who shout loudest', so he has appointed a European marketing manager to keep the agents up to scratch.

The main strand of the strategy at the moment is to open up the US market. Franks is convinced that Ion Tech could do a great deal better in America than it has done so far and, when I saw him in autumn 1982, he was exploring the possibility of opening up his own office in the US.

A significant presence in America will also help in the domestic market, Franks believes, because 'UK companies won't accept anything if it hasn't been done in the US.' This criticism of established British companies, that they tend to judge innovations and technological advances in terms of whether or not they were developed in America, crops up elsewhere in this book. It is a sad reflection of the deep-seated lack of national self-confidence in British industry which, hopefully, the appearance over the next decade or so of vigorous, medium-sized companies like Ion Tech will help to correct.

When confronted by what seemed to me to be the awesome technology being deployed at Ion Tech and Astron, it came as something of a surprise to find that of the 66 people working at the two sites (46 at Ion Tech and 20 at Astron) only one, Dr Franks himself, had a PhD. 'But I have some pretty good BScs,' Franks replied, and he went on to explain that although 20 per cent of sales revenue of the two companies was spent on what would conventionally be described as 'Research and Development', the vast bulk of this money was for development work.

As we have seen, saddle-field and X-ray optics technology came to Franks from a single government laboratory which is still a close collaborator, via the NRDC.

Franks is now making contact with universities such as Birmingham where work is being conducted on specimen thinning techniques. In a co-operative venture with the government and the University of Surrey, Ion Tech has provided some of its hardware in return for access to the results of an important semiconductor research project. Links are also being forged with the Middlesex Polytechnic.

'We get the "R" done there and we do the "D" ourselves,' says Franks. 'Our job is to develop marketable products.'

One of the things that has emerged from these seven company studies is that few of the entrepreneurs involved have had a very clear idea of a long-term business strategy.

Instead, they have tended to react to events and opportunities as they have come along. They seem to regard themselves and their companies as free-roving entities, committed to a more or less circumscribed technological area, but always ready to explore new applications and new markets.

Joe Franks, with a slightly studied diffidence, speaks of the company 'still being here by Christmas'. Though he recognises the growth potential of the markets his two companies serve, he is not convinced that he will, in the event, share fully in that growth.

His decision to press ahead with Astron appears to have been based not on a conviction that he will succeed but on the belief that his chances of succeeding are reasonably good. He has some strong cards like his technological lead, backing from powerful friends like the NRDC and MBIF, the excellence of his engineering team and his own intimacy with both the technology and the market. Armed with these strengths, he intends to take his chances and trust to a modicum of luck.

This characteristic lack of detailed planning and of intensive market research is, I believe, one of the great strengths of small companies during periods of rapid technological advance. Because small companies cannot afford to investigate in detail every aspect of a business proposition or opportunity, they must perforce rely on the instincts and business acumen of their proprietors. This endows them with a flexibility and a speed of reaction time which tends to be lost as companies grow larger. Small companies make mistakes of course, probably more per head than large companies do, but that is mostly because they take more decisions.

Even in normal times it is by no means clear that long deliberation, backed up with intensive investigation of every conceivable factor, is a superior decision-making procedure to the casual, off-the-cuff style of the entrepreneur. During times of rapid change the heavy-footed large company procedure becomes even more dubious. Rapid change means that the unknowns in the decision-making calculus are extremely significant. More and more time and effort have to be devoted to assessing the worth or otherwise of an investment proposition and by the time the decision is finally made there is a good chance that it will have been pre-empted by someone else or be simply out of date.

Entrepreneurs, the successful ones anyway, appear to be better at coping with change than the hydra-headed committees which run the large companies. They find change stimulating rather than problematical. But, as in the case of Joe Franks, the short horizon they perceive for their company does not prevent them from acquiring a clear view of the big picture – the directions in which the industry they operate in is moving.

9

Dr Tom Melling and Structural Dynamics

The story of Structural Dynamics is a classic tragedy. It involves, as Aristotle required, 'an action that is serious and also, as having magnitude, complete in itself'. The protagonist is 'a man not pre-eminently virtuous and just, whose misfortune, however, is brought upon him not by vice and depravity but by some error of judgment.'

The story also illustrates that in certain industries at certain times, small companies which wish to be larger may be required to put their lives on the line. Tom Melling, the hero of this tale, believes that some companies are simply incapable of growing at the steady pace their bank managers and accountants would like.

He argues that in certain industries, including the industry Structural Dynamics operated in, the business is simply too 'chunky' to accumulate gradually. You can pick up the odd bit of work here and there, but a company will only grow if it is prepared to go for the big contracts when they come along as they inevitably do in the offshore engineering world at irregular but relatively frequent intervals. In this sort of industry, dominated by a few large companies, small firms competing with new technology are forced to grow by a series of quantum jumps. Risks attend each jump. If the jump pays off then the company is one step nearer to the point where it is large enough to survive a crisis. If it does not pay off, then the company is dead.

Structural Dynamics experienced quantum jumps of both kinds.

Tom Melling was born in Ormskirk on 7 July 1942. He attended the Burscough Methodist School and at first seemed to be a boy of no more than average intelligence, claiming middle to low-order marks in most subjects. But towards the end of his time in primary education there was an intellectual awakening and he moved, at the age of 13, to the top of the class. He went on to Southport Technical College where he took good 'A' levels in maths, further maths and physics. He completed the first stage of his higher education with three years at Hull University reading physics.

In 1963, at the age of 21, he joined David Brown Gearing as a research engineer. His work at DBG, though it proved insufficiently stimulating to retain his interest for long, laid the foundations for his subsequent development as an engineer. He carried out research into noise vibration and he began to realise how difficult and at the same time how interesting the area was. He became hungry for more knowledge.

In 1965, at the NAVREX exhibition in London, he was attracted to the stand of Southampton University's Institute of Sound and Vibration Research (ISVR). It was what he had been looking for.

He applied for a position on a one-year MSc course and was accepted; no money though – the Science Research Council (now the Science and Engineering Research Council) was fully committed. There was no more cash for further postgraduate grants. But Melling was not to be put off by what in those days of optimism and prosperity seemed the trivial matter of finance. Tom had been earning £1,050 a year at DBG, which was a good salary for a 23-year-old by the standards of the day. He had no responsibilities though, and he was confident enough in his own abilities by then to be sanguine about the prospects for getting a job after the MSc course was finished. He and his new wife Ann travelled to Southampton, intending to live off what she could earn as a secretary.

Three months later Melling got lucky; on the strength of his chosen specialisation, he won a Rolls-Royce studentship. Tom Melling says everyone should be forcibly kicked out of university after their first degree. He believes the two years he spent at DBG were what gave him the hunger for research and the problem-solving approach to engineering which was to stand him in such good stead later.

His MSc thesis, published in March 1967, was entitled 'The acoustic behaviour of a porous material in the presence of low Mach number flow and high intensity sound waves'. It was directly relevant to the intense R&D programme Rolls-Royce was then engaged in – a programme that was to lead to the financial collapse of the company two years later and, soon after that, to the emergence of the RB211 aero-engine. Rolls-Royce was pleased with Melling's work and offered to finance his PhD. Once again the arrangement involved no obligation on Tom to join R-R afterwards, and once again the results of his work fed directly into the RB211 programme.

During the three-year course Melling's attention was focussed on the 'non-linear behaviour of acoustic absorbers'. He developed new techniques for measuring impedances and he designed special test facilities for measuring the behaviour of materials, especially perforated materials, under severe conditions. The course finished in 1970 but, like innumerable postgraduates of Melling's day and of subsequent days too, it took him a while to write up his work. He did not receive his doctorate until 1972.

The main reason for the delay was that as soon as the three PhD years were up Melling joined the Wolfson Unit, the commercial consultancy arm attached to the ISVR, as a full-time consultant. The job was well paid and involved quite a bit of high-living. He worked on hovercraft, kept in touch with Rolls-Royce and travelled widely, to America, Germany, Belgium and elsewhere.

Melling stayed at the Wolfson Unit for three years, gaining valuable experience, establishing a reputation for himself and, in his spare time, writing up his thesis.

In 1973 he received two offers. The first came as a result of a job he had been doing at the Wolfson for the Whitbread brewing group on a new bottling plant. He was invited to join the firm of architects who were designing the building. More or less simultaneously he was approached by a group of former Wolfson Unit colleagues who had recently broken away to set up their own company, Acoustic Technology Limited (ATL).

He pondered briefly and decided to join ATL. Within a short time he was appointed the company's technical director and was given a 7½ per cent stake in the company. It was soon after that when Melling's entrepreneurial instincts first became apparent. The development of the North Sea oil province was beginning to get under way in earnest by then. A consortium led by Chevron of the US and including ICI and a small independent company called London and Scottish Marine Oil (LASMO) had just discovered the giant Ninian field.

Melling's idea was for ATL to offer structural analysis and computer simulation services for offshore rigs and platforms. He put the notion to his fellow directors, Dick Davis and Derek Goodwin. They liked it and it was decided to form a new company to act as a vehicle for the diversification. It was called Structural Dynamics (Offshore). Goodwin took 10 per cent of the equity and Melling and Davis shared the rest between them.

Almost immediately SD won a £30,000 contract from Chevron, via the Lummus engineering consultancy company, to analyse the effects of vibration on the topsides of the planned Ninian production platform. The task was to assess the vibration induced by a machine working in a relatively elastic structure like a large oil platform.

But then came the parting of the ways. A serious row broke out between the three ATL directors and it became obvious that they could no longer work together. Goodwin left to set up Noise Reduction Limited, a fourth man, Robin Monk, established Acoustic and Vibration Technology Limited, Davis stayed with ATL and Melling shifted over full-time to Structural Dynamics (Offshore). As part of the deal, Davis swapped his 45 per cent of SD for Melling's 7½ per cent of the then considerably larger ATL.

So, at the age of 33, Tom Melling found himself the owner of 90 per cent of a young, high-technology company with its sights set on providing a whole range of services to the booming North Sea oil industry. His endowment was the Chevron contract, four people he took with him from ATL, good contacts in the industry and a collection of ideas about structural engineering which were to prove both powerful and lucrative.

The first thing he did was to hire a terminal and lease time on a computer. He then established the company in a small suite of offices. He remained on friendly terms with the university and his former colleagues at the ISVR, but the relationship was different from then on because SD became, to an increasing extent, a direct competitor of the Wolfson Unit.

Melling and friends were fortunate in those early days to have Chevron/Lummus as their first customer. The US oil group was an appreciative client and a good payer. The SD people were quite cash-rich – so much so that they were in a position to apply for shares at the time of LASMO's flotation on the London Stock Exchange, and to sell them on at a fat profit – an operation known in the City as 'stagging' a new issue.

SD was in the business of providing insurance policies for very substantial companies embarking on very expensive projects which involved extremely large structures. In those days the North Sea province was setting new standards in terms of both expense and the scale of engineering. SD could help the operators to anticipate engineering problems at the design stage or to monitor stresses, and diagnose problems, once the rigs and platforms had been built.

Though SD's main interest was in offshore structures, there were other contracts too, like noise analysis for a US bottling plant and a study of turbo-generator foundations for the Lonrho-financed Kenana Sugar project in the Sudan. And there was also a long-running contract with Thermoskyships, later to become Airship Industries, of which more later.

As the company grew, new opportunities arose. There was a natural progression from analysis to measurement and from there to the development of products. Tom Melling was not convinced that the North Sea oil boom would continue indefinitely and he was keen, from quite an early stage, to develop a series of machine condition monitoring units which could be sold into a wider market.

In 1976 the '(Offshore)' was dropped from the company name, reflecting Melling's wish to cast his net wider.

The chief competitors in those days were the company's own progenitor ATL, the large W. S. Atkins engineering consultancy in Epsom and Structural Dynamics Research Corporation of America.

One of the main problems encountered in building up the business was that computer-aided design, analysis and monitoring techniques were pretty new-fangled technology as far as most of the company's potential customers were concerned. As Tom Melling puts it, 'We were selling technology into a highly suspicious and conservative market.' The kind of methods SD was pioneering in the offshore industry were familiar enough when it came to aircraft and rockets, and to a lesser extent, motor cars, but they were quite new to offshore installations.

That meant that when Melling was touting for business, he was having to sell the technology itself as well as the ability of his company to use it. It was a question, he says, of winning the client's confidence. If you could impress him sufficiently with your track-record, your ability and your appearance of competence, then he would not worry too much about the technical details. One result of this was that each time you identified a new customer or market, and managed to sell the idea of doing things in a different way, then the competition tended to pile in after you.

SD started off with the Midland Bank. It was a natural choice because the Midland was ATL's bank and thus the local branch knew Tom Melling and had a rough idea of what the business was about.

But then, towards the end of SD's first full year of operations, a cash-flow crisis struck. Business was coming in thick and fast and profitability was excellent. When the accounts appeared for that year, sales were put at £201,000 and profits at £42,000 before tax. However, the 'chunkiness' of the business meant that working capital was needed to fund operations before phased payments began. In addition, SD was growing so fast that it soon needed more space. Melling found the accommodation he wanted at Carlton Crescent in Southampton but he was unable to raise the money to pay for it and to finance the computer system he also needed. He says that for the sort of money he wanted a bank needed to see three years of healthy figures before it would lend.

SD finally got a private mortgage for Carlton Crescent from a firm of solicitors in Fareham, but even when Melling waved a massive government contract under his bank manager's nose, he was unable to persuade him to extend the facilities needed to buy the computer system. The result was that on Christmas Day 1976 Melling was convinced that he had come to the end of the road. An important supplier was pressing hard for payment of a £1,000 bill and the bank was still refusing to increase the company's £10,000 overdraft.

So Melling turned to his accountant friend, Ian Wilder, whom he had met while still at ATL. He regards that meeting as an important event for SD. 'I met him just at the right time,' says Melling. 'He was teaching me a new language. I learned about costings and cash-flow from him and about financial planning and the right way to present proposals.'

At the time of the crisis Christmas, Wilder suggested that Melling might consider changing his bankers. He introduced him to Ron Amey, then manager of the Barclays Bank branch in Watford. The personal chemistry worked; Amey and Melling got on and the banker agreed to extend the overdraft facilities Melling needed. The crisis was over.

Barclays took fixed and floating charges on the company's assets but was otherwise flexible. Melling describes the difference between the Midland and Barclays during this crucial time in a characteristically personal way: 'Ron was prepared to take a flier.'

SD always exploited its bank facilities to the hilt and arranged separate loans for hardware purchases. Melling remembers some of the cash-flow projections he did for the bank to support requests for loans: 'You got back to the office and sat down and worked out what it all meant; "God!" you thought, "I've got to do £1.5 million this year" – it can be quite frightening.' But frightening or not, it did not prevent what Melling describes as the occasional 'spending binge', mostly on new computer equipment.

The trick was to go along to the bank towards the end of the financial year, show the bankers the likely profit and then tell them that unless they lent money for new computers and thus provided capital allowances to set against those profits, half the surplus would go down the drain to the tax man. The two most important contracts during the first life of Structural Dynamics were the Chevron/Lummus contract which played midwife at the company's birth and the *Alexander L. Kielland* contract which caused its untimely death.

In between there were other important milestones. The company was less than a year old when it won a contract from the Department of Energy's Offshore Supplies Office (OSO) which was eventually to be worth £1.2 million all told.

Oddly enough Tom Melling first heard that a big OSO contract was up for grabs when he was in Singapore trying to drum up export business. When he returned to Southampton he rang up the man in charge and was told that if he could get his tender ready within a week, it would be considered. The OSO, which is responsible amongst other things for improving safety standards in the offshore industry, wanted to conduct a full-scale integrity monitoring experiment on a North Sea oil production platform. It had chosen the Claymore field platform, then being built by the field's operator company, Occidental Petroleum.

The project involved the wiring up of the whole structure with transducers and other electronic sensors, feeding the information they gave into the computer, processing it with a tailor-made software package, and then displaying the result on a central monitoring unit on the platform itself.

Working round the clock, Melling and his team got their tender together and it was delivered, by hand, at the OSO's Glasgow headquarters, with just 15 minutes to spare. SD won the contract.

The work has been spread over several years and was not finally completed until after the collapse of Structural Dynamics, Mk 1. The project has aroused considerable interest in the offshore engineering world, both on the part of governments and oil companies, and there may yet be some follow-up business for Structural Dynamics, Mk 2 arising from it.

A system like this would not have prevented the *Alexander L. Kielland* drilling rig from capsizing in March 1980, but it would have given its occupants more warning of the impending disaster and that might have saved a good many of the 123 lives that were lost.

Another important contract was the one with Airship Industries, formerly Thermoskyships. It came through a chance meeting between SD's general manager and someone who knew Malcolm Wren quite well. Major Wren it was who, in partnership with David Potter, got the new airship project 'off-the-ground' so to speak.

Melling and Wren met and liked each other. Melling's professional interest was aroused by the airship idea and he did some work for Wren free-of-charge. Later, when Wren got together his Stock Exchange prospectus and raised his initial finance, a formal contract was signed. It involved a great deal of money, about £340,000 in all, and was excellent business for SD until Thermoskyships was re-structured into Airship Industries by Andrew Millar and Keith Wickenden, MP, and taken along a different path. At the end of the affair, when SD was reeling from the fatal blow inflicted by the Norwegians, there was a problem over payment by Airship Industries of an agreed £180,495 bill. It was the *coup de grâce.*

The OSO contract and the early stages of the Airship Industries contract put money into the bank. Melling says, 'I don't think you can afford to pass up contracts like that.' He reckons that if SD had been in the habit of picking and choosing contracts to suit the scale of the existing business it would not have had enough work to grow as fast as it did.

And you cannot always judge contract size accurately at the outset. Some contracts start off small and end up pretty large (the original Lummus contract, for example, grew from an initial £30,000 to over £200,000); others can begin by accounting for quite a fair slice of the existing business; and then, as more contracts are won, the exposure reduces.

The main thing as far as Melling was concerned was to keep moving. But he was aware of the need to stabilise the business and to prepare for the time when the North Sea oil boom began to run out of steam. That was why he backed electronics expert Tony Miles with £300,000 of internal development funding, to come up with the 'Perceptor' machinery monitoring unit.

There is now, perhaps not surprisingly in view of the events that took place in Norway during late 1980 and early 1981, a certain bitterness in Tom Melling. With hindsight he believes he should not have ploughed all the earnings back into the business but would have been better advised to salt a little away over the years in some tax haven. For there were rainy days ahead.

I first heard about Structural Dynamics in the late summer of 1980 when a brief press release was issued stating that Norwegian salvors Nicoverken Norge A/S, in partnership with SD Marine of Southampton, had won a contract from Stavanger

Drilling A/S, the owner of the stricken *Alexander L. Kielland* drilling rig cum 'flotel', to attempt a salvage operation.

It was the most prestigious salvage contract ever awarded. All the major salvors had tendered for the job. I decided to go down to Southampton and see what it was about this small, British company that had enabled it to elbow its way through the established groups in marine salvage and pick up the contract of the decade.

I was enormously impressed by what I saw down there and I came back and produced not an article but a eulogy. I wrote as if the *Kielland* was already right side up, that SD, having developed this brilliant new salvage technique, had already done the hard part and that the actual raising of the rig was a mere formality. I wrote of 'an awe-inspiring concentration of British brain power', of 'a constant state of intellectual excitement, boundless optimism and self-confidence' down at Carlton Crescent and I suggested that the righting of the *Kielland* would demonstrate 'the vigour and innovative power that is to be found in Britain's corporate undergrowth'.

The article was clearly 'wrong' in a number of ways. It made a completely inaccurate prediction about what the immediate future held in store for the *Kielland* and the implication that SD itself was a young company heading for fame and fortune proved totally erroneous.

But why was it wrong? Did I misjudge the technical ability of Melling and his team? Was I taken in by an appearance of commercial acumen that had never, in fact, existed? Did I mistake confidence for competence? Were the signs already there, for those able to read them, that Dr Melling and his colleagues were deluding themselves, and by association me, and that it was really evident by then that the *Kielland* contract would end in disaster? These questions are important because what if it had not ended in disaster? What if the *Kielland* had risen majestically out of the waters of the Gandsfjord the following month, precisely as planned and precisely on budget?

SD's reputation would have been enormously enhanced. Other major salvage contracts would have fallen into its hands. For the Kielland contract alone, the result would have been net profits of about £500,000 for three months' work, the opportunity to tender immediately for the contract to repair the rig and the probability of winning the repair contract. SD would have completed another quantum jump.

The difference between what might have been and what actually happened was made up, in this case, of a number of factors that linked together in a complex and completely unforeseeable way. The reader must decide whether the disastrous consequences of SD's confrontation with the *Alexander L. Kielland* were due largely to bad luck or largely to bad judgment.

The saga began in late 1979 when Alan Whittaker, an SD employee, suggested to Melling that the company should go for a share of the underwater market. Subsea well-completion systems were becoming popular at the time because although they involved more sophisticated technology, they offered the prospect of substantial savings in platform costs.

Whittaker foresaw good business in the monitoring of subsea plant and equipment and in the provision of computerised inspection systems. Melling liked the idea and a new company, SD Marine, was formed, with the parent company taking 50 per cent of the equity and Whittaker and a subsea specialist friend of his taking 50 per cent between them. Whittaker had good contacts in this area and when the idea of a *Kielland* salvage operation was mooted SD Marine was approached by Nicoverken Norge A/S (Nico) and was asked whether it could dream up a way of righting the rig without damaging it.

Nobody knew whether a righting would prove possible. Conventional salvage techniques are pretty crude and would have involved massive cranes and other lifting gear which would have subjected the *Kielland* structure to extremely high stresses. The chances were that the rig would have broken up altogether had normal methods been employed.

The owners were obviously anxious to get as much money back from the *Kielland* disaster as they could and since the oil exploration market was going through something of a boom period at the time, leading to a dire shortage of large, semi-submersible drilling rigs like the *Kielland*, the prospect of being able to right the rig and then repair it was very attractive.

Nico reasoned that the salvage consortium which came up with the plan that seemed to offer the best chance of a gentle, non-destructive righting operation would be well placed to win the contract. It was an exciting proposition for SD and a fascinating intellectual challenge. Melling and his team went away and thought about it. They had one of their characteristic brainstorming sessions and came up with a plan to right the rig without even touching it.

Broadly speaking the idea was to use the rig's own ballast tanks, most of which were still intact according to the contract specification, to turn it very slowly through 180°. Added buoyancy at critical points would be provided by sturdy flotation bags attached to the rig itself. The degree of buoyancy, and the process of trimming the buoyancy through the righting operation, would be closely monitored by computers. Ballast and buoyancy would be shifted gradually in pre-determined steps to avoid any rapid, high-stress movement which might cause the rig to break up.

Convinced that it was possible, Melling formed a joint company between Nico and SD Marine to which the parent company would become the main sub-contractor, and then they tendered for the contract. The SD men had convinced themselves that the novel technique would work through computer simulations, but the old problem of persuading potential customers unfamiliar with the new methods remained. It was decided, a week before the closing date for tenders, that they would have to show their potential customers something a little more substantial than reams of computer print-outs.

So they asked a little firm in Farnborough, which specialised in technical model making, to construct a scale model of the *Kielland* in perspex. The model was completed in five days at a cost of £1,000 and videotapes were made of it turning from upside-down to rightside-up in the test tank at Carlton Crescent. The presentation and tender documents cost over £30,000 and took four weeks to prepare.

The Nico/SD tender was the dark horse. No one outside SD, except, perhaps, one or two of its customers, dreamt that a small British company, with no experience in marine salvage, would be chosen. But as Tom Melling reasoned, size has got nothing to do with competence and not much to do with the relevance of the techniques SD was pioneering. The stricken *Kielland* was a massive object but, like everything else, it was subject to the natural laws of gravity and to the well-understood principles of fluid and structural dynamics. 'Why get uptight about the size?' was Melling's attitude.

After the tenders had been lodged there was a wait until the owners were in a position to draw up a short-list of three. SD was on it and was summoned to Norway to expand on its proposals.

Probably what attracted Stavanger Drilling most about the SD plan was the negligible risk it appeared to carry of a secondary disaster which might add to the death-toll of 123 lives when the rig had capsized the previous March. It seemed to the owners that salvage proposals which relied on brute force were not only less likely to succeed but were also much more dangerous for those involved than the gentle almost cajoling methods being proposed by SD. The idea of more deaths was anathema to them.

So the Nico/SD consortium won the contract with a tender price of £4.5 million. Melling felt quite relaxed about it. There did not seem to be much risk involved for SD. The company was quite cash-rich at the time and the contract with Stavanger Drilling seemed pretty watertight.

Melling estimated that the salvage operation would take three months to complete and that it would add £500,000 to that year's profits and would more than double that year's turnover, from the £3 million or so it would have reached otherwise to over £7 million. It was a classic Melling-style quantum jump. In one leap it would have SD knocking on the door of the big league which in Melling's book included companies with an annual turnover of more than £10 million.

The first task was to tow the rig very slowly, stress monitoring it all the way, from Karsto where it had been towed following the capsize to the deep but sheltered waters of the Gandsfjord. The voyage took four days. As soon as the *Kielland* arrived at Gandsfjorden, the project manager sent divers down to survey the structure, establish what sort of state it was in and to prepare the ballast tanks for the injection of buoyancy at the critical spots. They found that there were disturbingly large discrepancies between the actual state of the rig and its condition as specified in the tender and contract documents.

It was later estimated that there were 2,000 tonnes of water inside the structural members and the ballast tanks that simply should not have been there. This did not make the job impossible because the natural laws and principles of gravity and dynamics still applied, but it made the job very different from the one SD had prepared itself for. Most important, it promised to pose some very tricky problems at the crucial half-way point when the rig had to be swung through the 'deck vertical' position.

Undeterred, though perhaps a little uneasy by now, the SD team went away and did their sums all over again, taking into account as much of the extra weight as they knew about. The righting operation began a few weeks after the scheduled date and proceeded smoothly enough until the rig was approaching the 90° point. Then it stopped.

In retrospect Melling says he should have walked off then, claiming that this was not the job he had contracted for. Instead he and his consortium colleagues sat down with the insurers, the Norwegian Oil Risk Pool (NORP) and re-negotiated the contract. (NORP had taken over from Stavanger Drilling by then as the main contracting party.) It was evident that some extra buoyancy would be needed to tip the rig through the deck vertical position and the only way to provide that appeared to be by using lift barges whose cranes could take some of the weight at the high stress points. This would be expensive.

Eventually a new total contract figure of £5.5 million was agreed, leaving SD itself with the prospect of a somewhat smaller but still substantial profit.

But then problems of a quite unexpected kind began to develop. Norway was in a delicate political state at the time with a general election looming. The raising of the *Kielland* was a very visible and significant national event. The families of the victims of the original disaster were pressing for an inquiry and lodging compensation claims and there may have been one or two who would as soon have seen the rig sunk.

No one seems quite clear what the precise sequence of events was, but there was certainly a whole series of clandestine meetings between various parties. The Norwegian union movement is said to have put pressure on the government, though union leaders deny this, and there was a wrangle about jurisdiction between the Department of Energy and the Norwegian Coastal Directorate. There was even a suggestion that King Gustav himself became involved at one stage, although the particular context was not spelled out. There was talk of the rig being a danger to shipping and much discussion about the risks being run by divers and others involved in the righting operation. Whatever the precise details were, the result of all the toing and froing, arguing and lobbying was to turn what had originally been a reasonably straightforward business deal between the Nico/SD consortium and the *Kielland*'s owners into a full-blooded political issue.

On 20 November 1980 the Norwegian government ordered a halt to the righting operation, pending an investigation by a group of university professors into the methods being employed.

Since it was going to cost about £60,000 a day just to keep the rig where it was, the insurers were quite naturally anxious to establish which party would be responsible for these costs, especially as there was no precise time-scale for the investigation and no guarantee that the righting operation would be permitted to continue afterwards.

The government disavowed any responsibility for the extra costs arising from its decision, so the insurers terminated the Nico/SD contract on 28 November and negotiated another contract with SD to put the rig back down again. The de-righting operation was completed successfully on 11 December.

At this time SD's financial position, though fast becoming serious, was not yet critical. The progress payments had been coming in as each contract 'milestone' was passed and another large sum had been due at the righting which would have taken place, according to the salvor's schedules, about three days after the government stepped in.

But having completed the de-righting job, SD was becoming anxious about the costs it had committed for generators, pumps and scaffolding which would have been needed to complete the righting and then clean and weatherproof the rig. The consortium was obliged to begin litigation proceedings against NORP in an attempt to recover these costs and obtain full payment for work done. The case went to arbitration. The arbitration award, which Melling reckons was reasonable enough (roughly £500,000), was paid directly into the consortium company's bank account. It stayed there.

A creditors' committee, whose members were Norwegian, managed to freeze the account pending full distribution to them. SD, the consortium's largest creditor, could not touch its share.

Meanwhile, back home, Barclays Bank had become seriously concerned about SD's financial position and in March 1981 it asked accountants Ernst & Whinney to monitor the company's performance. The overdraft peaked at about £420,000. Tom Melling reckons the bank would have allowed him to try to trade out of his problems if he had managed to get that figure down to £200,000 or so. He says he could have done that easily enough if the money in that frozen bank account had been released and if Airship Industries had paid up in time.

Neither of these last chances came good and on 2 September 1981 Barclays announced the appointment of a Receiver, Nigel Hamilton of Ernst & Whinney. Tom Melling was on holiday at the time. Melling then entered a dark period in his life. He had been under great personal strain during the troubled righting operation, the re-negotiation of contracts, the freezing of the bank account and the arbitration proceedings; creditors both corporate and personal were breathing down his neck. He was depressed, angry and frightened. He began to drink heavily.

The main problem after Hamilton's appointment was that Melling felt powerless to do anything about the fate that had overwhelmed him and his company. SD was now being run by a stranger for the purpose of realising as much for its assets as possible, which was not at all like the way Melling had run it. Some of the staff, idle and dispirited, drifted away; others were made redundant.

But such was SD's reputation in its industry that about ten companies expressed interest in picking up what pieces were salvageable – they included Macdermott's, W. S. Atkins, Vickers, Seaforth Maritime and British Underwater Engineering. It soon became apparent that if there was to be a deal at all it would be along the lines of a slimmed-down, restructured company built around Tom Melling and what members of his technical team were left.

In the end Melling himself chose the purchaser, Palmer EaE, a loosely linked group of engineering companies run by a couple of entrepreneurs, Francis Holmes and Jeffrey Pike. Melling recovered slowly from the trauma of the collapse and began to put the business back on its feet. It was a question, more than anything else, of rebuilding the company's credibility.

He led the new Structural Dynamics into different markets, involving more systems work than previously, concentrating on the areas of control and data acquisition. An offshore capability was maintained but the company's centre of gravity began to drift onshore.

By the autumn of 1982 Melling was fully re-engaged. 'I think I've got it right again,' he told me in August. He was becoming interested in robotics and had found a number of new markets for the control and monitoring techniques that SD had deployed to such good effect for a while in the offshore industry.

Tom Melling regards himself primarily as a problem-solver: 'If someone has a problem, I can usually think of a way to solve it.' But he still feels cheated. 'I don't want to go down the receivership path again,' he said, 'especially when it's not my own bloody fault.'

During the period of SD's receivership personal animosity developed between Melling and the Receiver, Nigel Hamilton.

Relationships between entrepreneurs and receivers cannot be easy at the best of times. Imagine what it was like for Tom Melling. The company he had founded and built up from nothing into a substantial group goes wrong through, he believes, no fault of his own. The bank takes fright and appoints a receiver. Melling was feeling bad enough about the whole affair already and then some stranger moved in and took control.

Hamilton's responsibility was to Barclays Bank and the preferential creditors. He was required by the terms of his appointment and by company law to extract the best possible price for the remaining assets. He became incensed when Melling did a deal with Palmer EaE behind his back. Negotiations with another suitor, who had actually been introduced to Hamilton by Melling himself, were at an advanced stage.

The accountant felt Melling had behaved 'irresponsibly' and said so. 'He cut the ground from under our feet,' Hamilton said afterwards. 'He interfered with our attempts to get the best possible price.' Melling, in his heightened emotional state, positively relished the experience of striking back against what he regarded as the predatory establishment. He said of his run-in with Hamilton: 'I stuffed him.'

It was not, of course, the fault of Barclays Bank or of Nigel Hamilton that SD had fallen victim to Norwegian circumstances. On the other hand, it is not hard to see why Melling had become so bitter by then and so prone to lash out at anyone or anything associated with his company's failure.

Hamilton acknowledges that SD 'had some good technical ideas'. He believes the *Kielland* 'probably could have been righted' by Melling and his colleagues. He says, 'Dr Melling was the victim of a political decision not to right the *Kielland*. He was a bit unlucky.' But Hamilton also believes that Melling's troubles were partly self-inflicted. He suggests the company had invested too much time and effort in one large contract, that it had spent too much money developing the 'Perceptor' monitoring unit and that it had 'no adequate financial management'.

He also believes that mistakes were made during the Kielland affair itself. 'He' (Melling) 'didn't have control in Norway. He was not aware of his partner's tax position. He was too optimistic about the prospects for getting the money back. He was not sufficiently aware of the fact that in disputes involving foreign companies, charity always begins at home.'

He says that if Melling had not stuck out so firmly for the whole of the Airship Industries bill and had instead reached a settlement, and if the money owed to SD in the frozen bank account had been paid promptly, Structural Dynamics might have survived.

It seems to me that this sort of judgment of bust companies relies so much on hindsight that it is practically useless. Small, young companies, the salt of tomorrow's economy, are started on a wish and a prayer and spend much of their early lives reaching for the moon while walking a tightrope. The fact is that most of them fall off.

To say that SD failed because it was inadequately funded or because Melling spent too much on developing a new product, or because he was prepared to give too little ground in a dispute or because he did not understand the Norwegians, is like saying that the *Titanic* sunk because her hull was not strong enough to survive a collision with a very large iceberg.

The fact of the matter, as I see it, is that Structural Dynamics and the *Titanic* foundered on the same thing – plain bad luck.

Epilogue

Tom Melling's involvement with Palmer EaE ceased in December, 1982. Francis Holmes was running the group on his own by then and his ideas about the direction in which the reformed Structural Dynamics should be moving began to diverge seriously from Melling's own preferences.

Melling wanted to pursue the innovative, high-technology path while Holmes wished to concentrate on the less glamorous but still lucrative maintenance market. That, at least, was how Holmes explained the parting of the ways. Melling's account was characteristically blunter; 'he wanted me out' was how SD's founder put it.

But the parting was amicable enough. Holmes paid a fair price for Melling's shares and there is little evidence of bitterness on either side.

Tom Melling looked around for a while, received several offers, and then decided to throw his lot in with the small, USM-quoted high-technology group Anglo Nordic. The corporate vehicle formed around him was christened Fielden Inspections Limited and was based on a number of important licences Melling had acquired exclusively from US group General Dynamics in the area of non-destructive testing.

PART III

Business culture

10
With the current

To predict as I have done that small, high-technology companies will replace giant corporations as the dominant corporate species, and then to propose that such companies should be given preferential treatment, would be both illogical and specious. It would be tantamount to the Marxist exhortation: 'Help to bring about the inevitable.'

The inevitability of a development implies nothing about its desirability and in any case, attempts to encourage or obstruct such a development will, by definition, prove fruitless in the long run. To be convinced of this one only has to look at the history of the British Steel Corporation over the past ten years. But that 'long run' qualification is important. The speed with which our economy adapts to the requirements of effective, high-technology operation is crucial.

I have suggested that competition in these new circumstances has more to do with technological lead than with traditional economies of scale and that this is because the most important aspect of technological advance these days is its accelerating speed.

The pace of advance may stabilise within a few decades, though I doubt it, but by that time the corporate landscape will have changed utterly. We cannot wait for a possible deceleration. We have to deal with the speed now. The way to deal with it, of course, is to give in to it; to become part of it, to be one of Schumpeter's 'gales of creative destruction' as the Japanese economy has been in the Western world.

I believe the previous seven chapters have helped to show that the British economy has the potential to be such a gale, but the two crucial ingredients, the entrepreneurial spirit and scientific originality, are constrained in Britain. This constraint consists of a collection of obstacles barring our way towards a modern, flexible economy able to respond swiftly to the exigencies of rapid technological advance.

The cult of the loner

British entrepreneurs are often their own worst enemies. Those who do make the break from our establishments usually do so alone. They acquire close friends and colleagues, but they tend to bear the risks and responsibilities on their own shoulders.

This is reflected in a reluctance to part with equity (shares in the company), just one of a number of striking contrasts with the entrepreneurial tradition in America.

British entrepreneurs appear to prefer bank finance to permanent capital injections, even during periods of historically high interest rates. Part of the reason for this is undoubtedly the lack of a mature venture-capital market in Britain (see below) but by the same token one could attribute that same lack to the preference for loan finance – the two attitudes feed on each other.

We have seen in the previous chapters that entrepreneurial partnerships, which are gradually becoming more common here, can lend great strength to a new company. We have also seen that 'solus' entrepreneurs can feel the need for partners some time after they form their companies. This need may be conscious and articulated or it can be readily inferred from such features as chronic undercapitalisation or inadequate growth. Loan finance is bank finance and banks are, by and large as the previous chapters have shown, fairweather friends. Entrepreneurs need more steadfast allies than that and they will normally only find them by surrendering equity.

The friends can be literally friends or they can be venture capitalists prepared not only to put up money in return for equity but prepared also to take an active part in the running and development of the business. Such venture capitalism is known in America as 'hands on' or 'pro-active' and it is still much too rare in Britain, though thankfully it is no longer non-existent. Another reason for the loneliness of the British entrepreneur may be the fact that there are not so many of them about and that they have therefore had to spread themselves more thinly over the available opportunities.

If that is the case it can have nothing to do with a natural, national propensity to generate fewer entrepreneurs per thousand head of population than America – our economic history shows no sign of such an endemic weakness.

More likely, the supply of British entrepreneurs is being restricted by institutional and cultural factors. I shall deal with the importance of culture in the final chapter; for the moment I want to delve a little into history, to illustrate a more immediate and more remediable constriction on the supply of entrepreneurs.

The Tontine trap

In the middle of the seventeenth century a Neapolitan banker called Lorenzo Tonti initiated a financial scheme in France that came to be known, after the name of its inventor, as a 'Tontine'.

The idea was that a number of people should subscribe money to a common fund and that each should receive thereafter an annuity from the fund for the rest of his or her life. The total sum dispensed each year remained the same but the sums received by the participants increased as their numbers were reduced by death, until the point when the last survivor received the whole of the annuity. The Oxford Dictionary cites the case of one such eighteenth-century investor: 'This gentlewoman had ventured 300 livres in each Tontine; and in the last year of her life she had for her annuity . . . about 3,600 livres.' The Tontine is a mixture of prudent provision for one's old age and outright gambling on one's own longevity relative to that of other members of the scheme. It contains an element of insurance and a motivation for murder.

The Tontine came to hold a morbid fascination for young officers in the armies of warring nation states in Europe. Before what promised to be a bloody campaign, groups of them would pool their wealth in the expectation that those who survived, though bereft of their friends, would at least enjoy a more substantial income. For them it was a straightforward gamble on life or death, rather like Russian Roulette which would be invented later.

The idea of the Tontine has proved extremely durable and over the past three centuries it has spawned a number of variations on the same theme.

One such Tontine-variant involves annual subscriptions to the sinking fund by each member until a particular point is reached when members cease paying into the fund and start receiving their annuities from it. In this version, the annuities received by survivors are swollen in two ways – by the death of others receiving payments and by the early departure from the scheme of those who are still subscribing to the fund.

Under this sort of arrangement the motivation for murder survives in the second stage of the scheme and in addition there is a powerful incentive to stay in the scheme until the point at which subscriptions to the fund cease and payments from it begin. Nowadays, these two-part Tontines are more commonly known as funded pension schemes. The idea of pensions is so unutterably respectable, almost tediously so for those much below the age of 40, that it is easy to overlook that deep-seated strand of viciousness that runs through the idea of the funded pension scheme.

These latter-day Tontines imprison people in their jobs, forcing them to reject new opportunities and challenges that might appear in the second half of their working lives. Worse, they cause the 40- to 65-year-olds to become blind to opportunity. They become psychologically incapacitated by the growing investment in their pension schemes from even recognising opportunities when they do appear. The result of this is that about the only significant source of business experience available to young companies are the ranks of retired people – those who have crossed the threshold between the two parts of the Tontine.

I'm over-stating the case of course. Early leavers from funded schemes do get some money back, but not nearly as much *pro rata* as they would have done had they stayed until retirement age.

The problem of pension-fund early leavers is recognised, but it remains. It angers and frustrates people in their 40s and early 50s before they become reconciled to working out their time until retirement. It also robs the economy of a mobile army of experienced and adventurous men and women who could, in other circumstances, have made an invaluable contribution to the re-structuring of industry.

As far as I can see there are three possible solutions to the problem, two of which involve legislation. The first is to outlaw privately funded schemes altogether and force everyone to become members of a single state scheme.

Secondly, pension fund trustees could be required by statute to disburse fair shares to early leavers. This would be vigorously opposed by the corporate sector because it would involve much larger employer contributions to pension funds to maintain the same level of pensions.

Thirdly, those who wish to keep their options open as they grow older could club together and establish their own pension fund to which they would contribute throughout their working lives, irrespective of where and for whom they might be working at any one time.

The mundane entrepreneur

It is generally recognised in America that an important stimulus to the supply of entrepreneurs over the past two decades or so has been the example set by other conspicuously successful entrepreneurs. There have been, in places like Silicon Valley and the environs of the Massachusetts Institute of Technology (MIT) in Boston, the visible presence of 'role models' for would-be entrepreneurs.

If talented and ambitious young people see healthy new businesses growing up around them in a well-defined geographical area operating in a familiar and equally well-defined technology, 'going-it-alone' or in partnership with one or two friends becomes a much more credible option. From being courageous, foolhardy, arrogant, quixotic or downright stupid, the idea of setting up in business on one's own account becomes almost mundane – an eminently reasonable way of resolving the problem of what to do with one's life.

There is no reason to suppose that the power of example

works any less strongly in Britain. As we have seen, the area surrounding Cambridge University now exhibits some of the qualities of a Silicon Valley-type concentration of role models. There is also a growing concentration of high-technology companies strung out down the so-called 'Western Corridor' along either side of the M4 Motorway and there has been a remarkable proliferation of high-technology companies in parts of Scotland.

But we are still several years behind America in the development of large areas where the idea of going-it-alone has become mundane – where, if you like, the concentration of role models has reached critical mass.

Part of the reason for this is that until quite recently we have lacked in Britain what is known as an 'over-the-counter' share market. The Americans have had a large and sophisticated OTC market for twenty years or more, and a number of successful high-technology companies have raised substantial sums of money on it.

The British Stock Exchange, despite the urgings of many of its own members, steadfastly set itself against the establishment of a similar market here until at last the 'Unlisted Securities Market' was opened with something less than whole-hearted enthusiasm by the Stock Exchange in late 1980. The features which distinguish the USM from the main market are several: it costs less to get a USM quote than a full listing, it is not necessary for a company to have such a long track-record, companies do not have to surrender so much of the equity (the main market requires a minimum of 25 per cent of the equity to be traded to ensure 'orderly market conditions'), the prospectus does not have to be so comprehensive.

The existence of the USM lowers the threshold of public quotation – it permits entrepreneurs to win access to a large source of capital considerably earlier than would otherwise be possible. For investors in small, high-technology companies, the USM provides a more immediate 'exit route', permitting the adoption of more flexible venture-capital investment strategies. Investment in USM stocks is undeniably more risky than investment in main market companies, but the evidence to date suggests that the potential for capital gain is also considerably greater.

At a time of rapid technological advance, when financial resources need to be shifted from the old staple industries to the new technology-driven companies, a market of this kind is an essential catalyst. The Stock Exchange has, in my view, done the economy a great disservice by delaying the introduction of the USM for so long. It should have happened at least fifteen years earlier. If it had, there would now be a much larger supply of role models in this country to inspire others to take the entrepreneurial plunge.

A USM quote can turn an entrepreneur into a multimillionaire, on paper at least, almost overnight. Such a flotation attracts publicity and helps to make the idea of the wealthy, self-made man or woman, still in their 30s or 40s, more mundane.

It is ironic that the reluctance of the British Stock Exchange to introduce such a market is the result of its desperate desire to remain independent and free from statutory regulation. The SE, appalled by the idea of statutory control exercised through the equivalent of America's Securities and Exchange Commission, has been ultra-conservative in its market development policies, fearful that a less regulated market like the USM will generate just those abuses and scandals that will finally persuade government to impose statutory control. Whatever the rights and wrongs of statutory versus self-regulation, the SE's fear of outside control must rank as a serious obstacle towards the highly flexible capital markets we will need in the decades ahead. If the only cure for the paranoia is to give it substance – to impose statutory regulation – then that is a price that will have to be paid.

The venture capitalists

The retarded development of British capital markets is also evident in what I call the 'pre-quoted sector' – the buying and selling of shares in companies before they 'go public' on the USM or the main market. This is the realm of the venture capitalists, the 'all-weather' friends of the entrepreneur referred to earlier.

I suspect that one of the more important reasons for slow development here may have been the fate of a company we met in an earlier chapter, Spey Investments. Spey was founded in 1967 by financial journalist cum merchant banker Charles Gordon. It was a response to a problem encountered in all markets where there are large buyers and sellers.

By the late 1960s the growing power of Britain's private and public-sector pension funds and insurance companies, desperately seeking profitable resting places for their £600 million a year cash inflows, was beginning to distort the workings of the stock market. Institutional fund managers were finding that whenever they wanted to buy or sell shares, their substantial presence in the market forced prices against them. Their buying orders pushed prices upwards, robbing them of profit opportunities and their selling orders thrust prices downwards, generating self-inflicted losses.

Gordon's idea was that a large investment fund, focussed on unquoted companies where the market forces were far less significant, offered the opportunity of substantial profits. It is this quality of the pre-quoted sector that has attracted so much contemporary investment interest in private companies.

But Gordon knew that the problem with young, unquoted companies was that the entrepreneurs who ran them were relatively inexperienced. Because of the lack of a ready exit route at the time, in the form of the USM, investments had to be closely managed if risks were to be reduced to acceptable levels. The institutions were neither equipped nor inclined to adopt such a 'hands-on' approach to their investments, so they eschewed the pre-quoted sector, despite its other attractions.

Spey represented a solution to this dilemma. Gordon proposed to a number of private-sector pension fund managers that they should put money into his company and he should gather around him a team of highly experienced and respected managers who would identify promising young companies, invest money in them and then get intimately involved with their management and development. It is a tribute to Gordon's powers of persuasion that he recruited to the Spey cause not only £50 million worth of institutional backing plus the promise of a great deal more if things went well, but also the services of such men as Sir Paul Chambers, former chairman of ICI (and the then chairman of Royal Insurance), Sir Julian Salmon, ex-chairman of J. Lyons, Jasper Knight, who retired early as finance director of Unilever, Sir Joseph Lockwood and a number of other senior industrialists and fund managers.

Those who wrote the history of Spey's rise and fall attributed the adventure to Gordon's dazzling charm and infectious enthusiasm. He was the magician at the centre of a massive commitment of cash by the institutions and, perhaps more importantly, a commitment of time and energy on the part of senior and established business figures. He was, so the argument went, aided in this campaign of dazzlement and persuasion by his wife, prima ballerina Nadia Nerina. It was her style and elegance, coupled with Gordon's personal magnetism and lavish way of life, rather than the power of his ideas, which had seduced the institutions and the big names.

That, at least, was the way the establishment covered its tracks. The Spey Investments débâcle was put down to mesmerism, pure and simple. The big names and the big money had been duped. It was emphatically not a sign that the establishment itself had made an error of judgment.

Everything started well. In the first full year of operations to June, 1969, Spey recorded profits of £150,000 before unconsolidated losses of £93,000 and a dividend pay-out of £54,000. During 1970 Gordon got moving in earnest, buying Allied Land for £7 million, Goulston Discount for £4.6 million, a half-share in National Car Parks for £4.6 million and, in October 1970, Hallmark Securities for a hefty £20 million.

In retrospect it is clear that by then Gordon himself had become the victim of the dazzlement of other magicians who were laying the foundations of the property and fringe-banking boom soon to become bust. He became deeply involved in property through Spey-Westmoreland in partnership with Boris ('Bobby') Marmor (the ill-fated Brighton Marina venture was one of the larger projects) and he acquired the wish to establish Spey as a major investment banking concern. To this end he put Hallmarket's subsidiary Twentieth Century Banking together with Goulston to form Spey Finance. That was in April 1971. In the same month Jasper Knight, who had become chairman of Spey's venture-capital subsidiary Warwick Securities the previous October, resigned. Unilever, which had originally backed Spey with pension-fund money on Knight's recommendation, announced the phased withdrawal from Spey of its £5 million investment.

That was the beginning of the end. Rows broke out between the industrialists involved. Some were highly critical of Knight's defection which had exposed so cruelly the essential fragility of the Spey idea. One of Knight's former Spey colleagues said: 'It was a club and would only work if we all acted together.'

There was a board re-shuffle in June, establishment figures were called in to 'sort out the mess' and Gordon departed. But as it turned out Spey's shareholders lost very little money – peanuts compared to the huge sums that were to disappear later during the fringe banking crisis. Some shareholders made profits.

William Brandts, the merchant bank which ended up owning the rump of Spey, did quite well out of it. Three years later it was reported in the *Financial Times*' 'Men and Matters' diary column (23.5.74), '. . . and Brandts has got some viable investments, like the stakes in C. H. Industrials and Cray Electronics, plus a thriving (nearly £1 million profit) business in Carmen Curler, with the Sweetheart Plastics green field operation (jointly owned with Maryland Cup Corporation of America) just coming into profits. So perhaps Spey wasn't such a bad idea in the end.'

It is easy to be wise after the event, but it is at least arguable that had Spey's investors shown more patience and had Gordon's enthusiasms for property and banking been held in check by his illustrious partners, Spey Investments might have lived up to its early promise. It is not hard to imagine circumstances in which Spey might have injected real dynamism into Britain's high-technology sector in the crucial 1970s when so much money was chasing the chimeras of property and banking.

The effect of the Spey trauma is wearing off now, but the tradition of venture-capital investment by financial institutions, particularly by private-sector pension funds, still bears the scars. Direct venture-capital investment by British companies has also been affected. In the US, companies themselves account for over a fifth of total venture-capital investment. With one or two honourable exceptions, like Coats Patons and Pilkington

Brothers, established companies are conspicuous by their absence from the British venture-capital scene.

Another organisation that has helped to retard the development of a modern venture-capital market in Britain, and one that is still very much alive, is the Finance for Industry subsidiary, Industrial and Commercial Finance Corporation (ICFC). ICFC is the 'alibi' for the big banks when they are accused of not doing enough to help small companies. The bankers point across the river to ICFC's building in Waterloo and say 'You see there the headquarters of the world's largest venture-capital organisation. We own it.'

In fact ICFC masquerades as a venture-capital organisation. It is really a development capital organisation with a small venture-capital subsidiary called Technical Development Capital. It has many weaknesses. The most important is its excessive size which has seriously inhibited the development of a more diverse and thus a more flexible venture-capital market. It is an eminently suitable case for reference to the Monopolies and Mergers Commission.

Another side-effect of ICFC's size is that its unimaginative and anachronistic investment style has become the pattern for UK venture and development capital investment and this has probably contributed significantly to the 'loner' quality of the British entrepreneur referred to earlier.

Entrepreneurs do not like the ICFC for several reasons: because it charges too much for its loan finance (it is able to do so because of its quasi-monopoly position); because its equity stakes often appear to be no more than token gestures behind which the big banks extend the loan financing they prefer; because ICFC takes far too long to make up its mind about both initial financing and subsequent 'drip-feed' top-ups (a serious problem for high-technology companies operating in rapidly changing industries); because of its unwillingness or inability to provide moral and professional support in addition to finance; and because the way the ICFC is organised means that entrepreneurs who do get involved with the ICFC find themselves dealing mostly with young and relatively inexperienced people.

I make no apologies for singling out ICFC for this sort of criticism. It was estimated that in 1981 ICFC accounted for no less than 66 per cent of all venture and development capital invested in Britain. The organisation dominates the venture-capital market totally; it is essential that it should operate effectively. Its weaknesses, which are thus the weaknesses of the market as a whole, are most evident when its style is contrasted with the model of the successful American venture-capital funds of recent years.

These organisations are much smaller than the ICFC, they operate at arm's length from their source of finance, they spread their investments carefully over companies at different stages of their development, they do not feel obliged to 'get the money out of the door' as soon as possible, their fund managers have complete discretion and their senior executives are at pains to establish close personal and professional relationships with the entrepreneurs they back.

Whether it is sufficient to wait until natural selection erodes the baleful influence of the ICFC as it surely will, or whether the organisation needs to be split apart right away, I do not know, but something will have to be done about the ICFC.

The venture-capital market also needs more money. American experience has shown that in this area Say's Law, which states that supply creates its own demand, applies. It is simply not true to say that the more money invested in venture capital, the lower the quality of the investments. There is no fixed number of entrepreneurs – the supply is what economists call 'elastic'; the lower the price of going-it-alone (in terms of the cost of finance, the risk and the loneliness) the more people will try it. The explosion of the US venture-capital market in the mid-1970s was followed by dramatic improvements in the quality as well as the quantity of investments. Where should we look to for these new supplies of venture capital? Wealthy individuals have always been a good source on both sides of the Atlantic, but in Britain there has been another important, tax-efficient investment for such people – membership of Lloyd's of London, the international insurance market. Britain's admirable though flawed Business Startup Scheme, which was greatly extended in the 1983 budget to form the new Business Expansion Scheme, should help to divert some of the money now being invested in the international insurance market. However, the extension of the scheme to include all 'unquoted' companies may have the effect of shifting the specialist venture-capital funds away from their concentration on young or start-up companies towards a greater emphasis on investment in more mature and thus less risky enterprises.

Another under-exploited source of finance, and a source that is playing a significant role in the flourishing US venture-capital market, is the large company sector – the dinosaurs themselves.

Towards a federal system

If the corporate disintegration thesis is broadly correct, what should be the response of those running the dinosaur companies? There is nothing they can do to maintain the position of big business in the long run and I do not believe it would be sensible or in the interests of their shareholders to attempt such a defence. But that does not mean that there are no suitable adaptive strategies for big business.

There is already a tendency towards 'internal' disintegration within large corporations. Individual divisions are being given more autonomy in the belief that if they are freer from the bureaucratic restraints of head office they will be more productive. Many large companies are 'de-merging' – splitting up their divisions altogether rather than merely loosening the ties. Others are weeding out activities that are no longer considered part of the mainstream business and are selling them off, sometimes to the existing managers in so-called 'management buy-outs'.

These responses seem sensible, but they are passive. They acknowledge that the stream of efficiency is beginning to run away from large size, but they indicate no inclination to ride with it. There are two Chinese characters which translate roughly into the English word 'crisis'; one stands for danger and the other stands for opportunity. Big companies which become aware of the threat to their survival should be positive. They should explore actively the ways of making a virtue out of necessity. They should ask themselves why it is that small companies are beginning to win the initiative. If the answer seems to be that talented individuals, capable of coping with rapid change and keen to exploit the opportunities it offers, are more highly motivated and thus more creative when they are working for themselves, then a number of possible adaptive strategies should suggest themselves.

First of all, the managers of the big companies should make a deliberate effort to identify the peculiarly talented people, the potential scientist/entrepreneurs, in their own organisations. On occasions it will be possible to put together small teams and partnerships, perhaps including a scientist, an entrepreneur and a sympathetic accountant.

Having found these particularly creative nodes in their organisations, the big company managers should then invite the individuals concerned to set up their own companies under the umbrella of the corporation, on the understanding that when they have established a decent track-record the new company will be floated on the USM. The large companies will take their profit from their role of mid-wife by retaining a significant equity stake in the company. Quite how large this stake should be will depend on a number of factors such as how many individuals need to be given a piece of the action and what size that piece needs to be to retain the loyalty of the key people.

It will be important for the large companies not to insist on retaining control. They should recognise that if these people are not motivated sufficiently, they will leave and set up in competition. Big companies embarking on this federal approach to corporate re-structuring must keep in mind the fact that in doing so they are responding to a powerful evolutionary pressure. Their overall bargaining position is weak, however strong it might appear to be in individual cases.

Large organisations, having re-structured themselves along federal lines, can then go on the offensive. They should look around for the same sort of people and partnerships outside their groups and should offer them similar packages. They should become venture capitalists and should be aiming, in the long run, to turn themselves into large and well-diversified investment trusts.

The role of government

The advent of a modern, effectively disintegrated corporate sector is not something that can be brought about by the passage of a raft of legislation crafted by an enlightened government.

Governments should acknowledge that their role is largely passive and that their activities should be restricted to the removal of obstacles. Evolution will shape the nature and form of the industrial re-structuring; government can sometimes influence the speed with which the development unfolds.

An example of a problem that is within a government's area of competence is a difficulty encountered by more than one of the companies profiled in the earlier chapters – the length of time large organisations sometimes take to pay their bills. It is one of the axioms of cash-flow management that debtors should be kept to a minimum and creditors kept to a maximum – that one should demand payment from one's customers as quickly as possible and one should delay payment to one's suppliers for as long as possible. Axiom or not, such practices and principles hurt small companies. Because they are small they lack the market strength to resist such pressures and the result is that a significant part of the limited supplies of working capital available to them ends up in the coffers of their more powerful suppliers and customers.

One should always be reluctant to propose legislation as an answer to market imperfections, but this debtors'/creditors' abuse of market power is so widespread and so apparently incorrigible by other means that new law must be regarded as an option.

One of the most surprising things to emerge from these company studies is the apparent unimportance of high rates of income tax in the collection of motivations which generate entrepreneurial activity. The conventional wisdom is that high rates of personal taxation act as a powerful disincentive to enterprise. This may be the case with other kinds of entrepreneur, but my impression is that with the scientist/entrepreneurs, other motivations, apart from the desire for wealth, loom larger in the early stages. Later, as the entrepreneur grows older and begins to think of reaping his reward or of organising his succession, capital taxes on gains and transfers become matters of concern.

One should not take too literally the emphasis entrepreneurs themselves frequently put on their desire to be rich. Often it is merely a question of saying what is expected of them. British bankers and venture capitalists, most of whom are still relatively untutored in entrepreneurial psychology, are impressed by excessive displays of acquisitiveness. They take it as a sign that the entrepreneur is properly motivated and thus more likely to justify their faith in him. Indeed, almost invariably the first bit of advice an aspiring entrepreneur receives is, 'If your bank manager asks you why you want to start your own company, tell him that you want to make lots and lots of money.' If the conventional view of the greedy entrepreneur were broadly correct, such advice would be entirely superfluous.

It is corporate taxation that really matters in this area and I do not mean just conventional taxation. Corporation tax at its current rate of 52 per cent net of stock relief, seems to me to be quite reasonable; one could make out a case for saying that the allowances against corporation tax favour the large company because it may take a while for the small company to achieve profitability and thus be in a position to take advantage of the capital allowances; one could also suggest that it is wrong for large, loss-making companies to be permitted to carry those losses forward, year after year, to set against future tax liabilities. Given that a finite amount of corporate finance is available at any one time, such practices might be expected to favour the wrong kind of company.

But I do not want to make too much of this. A company should be regarded in the same way as a theory. Its business plan should not be judged fallacious as soon as losses appear. Losses are serious but if they are temporary, bad luck and the acknowledgment of tactical mistakes can be an adequate defence.

The real burden of corporate taxation is administrative. The system of taxes, contributions, regulations and reporting requirements deployed by government in this country is a blanket one; it makes no allowance for the fact that compliance costs bear more heavily on small companies. The entrepreneurs themselves do not appear to feel this point too strongly. The administrative chore of filling in forms and generally discharging a company's statutory duty to maintain a formal relationship with the state seems to be one of the few things entrepreneurs take for granted as a necessary evil.

But from the national point of view once again, it is clearly a waste of the entrepreneurial resource to require such people to spend too much of their time on clerical matters. More could be done to ensure that entrepreneurs are left free to spend as much time as possible being entrepreneurial.

Another area in which government may have a role is in the British way of corporate death. How easy do our institutions make it for a failed entrepreneur to 'pick himself up, dust himself down and start all over again'? When he finally struggles to his feet again, nursing a badly bruised ego, what lessons has he learned from his wretchedly gloomy conversations with the undertakers of the corporate world? Has he been convinced that failure is the ultimate sin by the constant repetition of words like 'irresponsible', 'over-trading', 'foolhardy' and by phrases such as 'breach of duty' and 'not fit to run a company' or is he permitted still to believe that it was better to have tried and failed than never to have tried at all?

If society has a tendency to say to the entrepreneur that his first failure must be his last, then a significant proportion of the entrepreneurial resource will go to waste. It would be better for everyone if we took a more particular view of corporate failure. Government could help by introducing arrangements along the lines of the American Chapter 11 bankruptcy proceedings which would permit troubled but viable companies to obtain temporary legal protection from their creditors.

The private sector could also contribute. Might it not be possible to establish a fund – let's call it the Casualty Ward Trust – whose stated purpose would be to identify small, high-technology companies in difficulties or even in receivership, to offer the entrepreneurs concerned a financial safety net in return for a sizeable equity stake and then to help them to trade out of their problems?

A high infant mortality rate is a cause for national concern and if the nation is wealthy enough it will be the inspiration for the investment in medical care needed to reduce it. For us as human beings the rough justice of natural selection is unacceptable for moral reasons. We have the power to reject that justice and we choose to exercise that power. We go further than that. We discriminate in favour of children for roughly the first quarter of their lives, feeding them, clothing them, educating them, caring for them and generally protecting them from the cut and thrust of the adult world until we deem them strong enough to fend for themselves. With companies the situation is precisely the reverse. More is spent on them as they grow, not less.

A corporate health service has evolved in Britain with a very substantial budget, but it is concerned almost exclusively with geriatric care. Our actions suggest that though we are in principle quite prepared to let natural selection work in the corporate world, there comes a time when companies cross over a threshold and become politically significant, when we feel obliged to interfere with the evolutionary mechanism.

One scientist/entrepreneur I know has proposed an alternative to this attitude. Generalising the idea of the 'sunrise' company working with new technology, he has suggested that there also exists a class of company that could be called 'sunset'. They are the ageing companies, working with yesterday's technology and by and large they are the main recipients of the resources dispensed by the corporate health service.

The entrepreneur proposes that the Queen and other VIP's who officiate at the openings of new factories and plants should also attend corporate funerals. Such ceremonies would be more sombre, but they need not lack dignity. There would be a sense of gratitude for services rendered and for a job well done – a feeling of sadness perhaps but also one of inevitability.

If agreement could be reached about which companies are of the 'sunset' type, one can imagine an industrial policy that favours closure above subsidy and deploys the resources released thereby in a major programme of education and re-training.

For when an economy is changing fundamentally and rapidly, the departure of labour from declining industries and their migration – preferably via education and re-training – to growing industries should be swift. In these circumstances there is a premium on high labour mobility just as there is on high entrepreneurial mobility. A corporate health service that favours the old at the expense of the young is resisting the evolutionary current.

Another kind of interference with the evolutionary process is exemplified by the work of the state-owned British Technology Group and its two subsidiaries, the National Enterprise Board (NEB) and National Research Development Corporation (NRDC).

The job of the NRDC is to ensure that the economic benefits that arise from state-funded research and development accrue to Britain. It is a necessary job; it would be wrong to permit such precious resources to be exported, free of charge, to foreign companies. But is an organisation like the NRDC the best means of achieving this goal? Might it not be better merely to insist that only British companies can apply for licences to exploit the results of state-funded research and to make it clear to each applicant that the licence will be revoked if the company ceases to be British?

The very existence of the NRDC tends to distort the workings of the market in ideas. It makes those doing research less mindful than they might otherwise be about the commercial potential of their work. They can tell themselves that they do not need to bother about that side of things because if their project does have commercial possibilities, the NRDC is bound to spot them and claim the benefit.

And on the other hand, companies which might otherwise be on the look-out for interesting research being conducted at British academic establishments can tell themselves that it is not worth spending too much time and money monitoring the work of scientists on the state pay-roll because that is precisely what the NRDC is for: 'No point in duplicating effort', the companies will argue, 'the NRDC spots things like the hovercraft that are only barely commercial. It's inconceivable that it will miss something really important.' Barring a controlled test of the NRDC's effect on the national innovation rate, perhaps involving the complete suspension of NRDC's activities and privileges for a period of say five years, it is not possible to come to an empirical view of the usefulness or otherwise to the country of the NRDC. The planned removal from the NRDC of first-refusal rights to the results of research financed by Britain's research councils should go some way towards revealing just how effective the NRDC has been over the past three decades or so. The worth of the NRDC can also be assessed in a different way. One can ask oneself general questions such as 'Is the NRDC the *sort* of organisation likely to spot the commercial possibilities in science with some regularity?' 'Is it the *sort* of organisation likely to attract the kind of people who are alert to commercial opportunity?' 'Can an organisation like the NRDC offer the right kind of inducements to its executives to make them act with sufficient boldness given that when someone else's money is involved it is invariably safer to say no to a proposition than to say yes?'

My answer to all these questions is 'No' – the NRDC does not strike me as being a naturally entrepreneurial organisation.

Even so, the NRDC might still on balance appear to be useful if it could be shown that, although not naturally entrepreneurial, it does at least have more flair in that department than British industry at large. It was partly concern that this might indeed be the case which led to the creation and the retention of the NEB and to the subsequent formation by the NEB of the Inmos microchip company and the Celltech biotechnology company. The NEB said to British business, 'You ignored standard chip-making and broadly-based biotechnology, presumably because you did not think there was any money to be made there. We think you were wrong.' The proof of these particular puddings will be in the profits or lack of them which Inmos and Celltech are earning in five or ten years.

So far the odds appear to be favouring the NEB. The reason for this is that the NEB has always recognised the importance of the entrepreneur. Inmos was set up in partnership with Dr Dick Petritz of the US and Dr Iann Barron of the UK, and the idea of Celltech was conceived by a highly entrepreneurial NEB executive, Gerard Fairtlough, now Celltech's managing director.

But other market imperfections are introduced by the creation of such 'nationalistic' companies for they are the result of the failure of large companies to involve themselves in certain areas. The sudden appearance of large, well-funded nationalistic companies can sometimes squash small companies trying to exploit those very opportunities their larger rivals have missed.

One can detect in the existence of institutions like the British Technology Group a general lack of national faith in British industry's ability to spot and exploit opportunities generated by rapid technological advance. This lack of faith is part of our business culture.

In the end, all these things, the flexibility of our capital markets, the enlightenment or otherwise of our bankers, the importunity of government agencies, the way we deal with corporate death, our generosity to the big and the old at the expense of the small and the new and our tendency to bind experienced people in their jobs with cords of gold – all these things reflect and comprise our business culture; they define the place that business occupies in the minds of the people.

11
The fourth factor

The American economist Israel Kirzner suggested that the entrepreneurial quality, what he called 'entrepreneurial alertness', is so important that it should be regarded as a fourth 'factor of production' alongside the three factors identified by classical economists: land, labour and capital. Kirzner went on to attempt the difficult task of incorporating this fourth factor into a new theory of the firm. He encountered a major difficulty: how to define the return on entrepreneurial alertness. The return on land is rent, the return on labour is the wage or salary, the return on capital is interest. If wages go up and rents and interest rates remain unchanged, there is a tendency, according to classical theory, for more capital and land to be brought into the system of production.

But what is it that has to go up to inspire an increase in entrepreneurial activity?

Before we look at Kirzner's answer, I want to try to provide some inkling of the economic effects of entrepreneurial activity. There are, of course, no figures which are obviously relevant; one has to make do with what statisticians call 'proxies' – variables which, though not concerned directly with the object of study, might be expected to change in parallel with it.

The US General Accounting Office (GAO) recently published a study of American firms backed by venture-capital funds during the 1970s. Let us assume that companies backed by venture-capital funds are run by entrepreneurs and let us also assume that the performance of these companies relative to the performance of other companies and the economy as a whole is indicative of the economic effect of entrepreneurial activity.

The GAO concluded that firms backed by venture-capital funds during the 1970s have had a disproportionately beneficial effect on the economy. The study covered 72 firms backed, in aggregate, by $209 million worth of venture-capital funding. By 1979 the companies were generating total sales of $6 billion a year, they were employing 130,000 people, they were billing an annual $900 million worth of exports and up to that point they had achieved, again in aggregate, a growth rate of 33 per cent a year.

Evidence of an even more anecdotal kind about the significance of the entrepreneurial quality is to be found in a study of management buy-outs published by UK public relations consultants Nicholas Mendes & Associates in November 1982. The study, conducted by the market research firm Ridmar, covered 19 West Midlands industrial companies, each of which had undertaken a management buy-out (the assumption here is that the management buy-out is a reflection of entrepreneurial activity).

Ridmar concluded that apart from the obvious benefits of corporate survival and the preservation of jobs (in most cases the alternative to the buy-out was liquidation), the 'bought-out' company changed for the better in a number of ways. There was 'enhanced performance by highly motivated and competent management buy-out teams, due to the incentives influencing them; greater flexibility as a result of shorter chains of command; more rapid response to changes in the business situation; increased loyalty and morale amongst employees – in the short term at any rate – resulting in greater efficiency.'

These two studies are far from being clear evidence of the effect of entrepreneurial activity but in my view they are evidence of a kind that entrepreneurs both create and save jobs, while making money for themselves.

But is the making of money the prime motivation of these people we call entrepreneurs? Kirzner assumed so; in his model entrepreneurial alertness is always with us but is only transformed into entrepreneurial activity when the alert entrepreneur spots an opportunity – notices what Kirzner calls 'concatenations of events, realised or prospective, which offer *pure gain*' (his italics).

Kirzner argued that since the opportunity to make a 'pure gain' is what evokes entrepreneurial activity, it is essential to ensure that the cloud of such opportunities which is being scanned constantly by alert entrepreneurs is made as dense as possible. He suggested that the best way to achieve this maximum density was to make markets as free as possible – to adopt what would nowadays be regarded as right-wing economic policies.

I am not convinced that the model of the entrepreneur motivated by pure gain is an accurate one. The scientist/entrepreneurs I know seem pretty ordinary people to me, rather more intelligent than average perhaps, but possessed of a fairly conventional outlook on life, except where business is concerned. Their distinguishing features in their chosen area of business are the clarity of their vision, their ability to spot opportunities where others see only problems, their extreme optimism and self-confidence and their extraordinary capacity for hard work.

They do not seem to me to be unusually acquisitive people. They are seldom plagued by pangs of conscience about the inequity that is in the world and they enjoy wealth when they achieve it but greed is not the mainspring of their motivation. If anything their wealth is more important for its symbolic value than for any material comfort it brings. It proves something to others. It is evidence to support an argument or a point of view.

And I believe that all seven profiles in Part Two support the view expressed by Steve Shirley that 'entrepreneurs are unemployable'. They do not like working for others; they find the politicking that takes place in large organisations irksome; they hate to be thwarted in the pursuit of their own ideas.

They seem to have a stronger sense of self than most. They are not prepared to take nearly so much for granted, preferring to build up their world view on the basis of personal rather than second-hand experience. It goes without saying that they are less risk-averse than average. They are ready to trust more to luck and, at the risk of appearing tautological, I would suggest that successful entrepreneurs are, in fact, luckier than most people, or perhaps it is just that they recognise the importance of luck and are willing to ride it. They are not long-term planners. The perspective of their original business plan may be quite extensive, but their management style is flexible. They are always on the look out for new opportunities.

They often become quite lonely and perhaps this is one of the reasons why entrepreneurial partnerships seem to be so successful. They need confidant(e)s and gurus from time to time; people to lean on and be encouraged by. They do not suffer fools gladly; on average they appear to be better endowed with a sense of humour than most. They have a rare ability to infect others with their energy and enthusiasms; they are keenly aware of the need to find good people and to keep them, even at the expense of altering their own plans and of giving away some equity.

Above all, scientist/entrepreneurs are extremely creative people; their ideas, and the effort they put into realising them, make space in which other people can do useful work. In my view they are the only effective antidote to the corrosive structural unemployment that is poisoning our society.

But there is no public approbation for the self-made man or woman. The heroes of our time are artists, sportsmen and sportswomen, film stars, television personalities, soldiers, union leaders, social reformers, politicians, writers and the occasional scientist or philosopher. It seems that there is no room in the modern pantheon of the admired for the entrepreneur and the businessman.

In a society still dominated by the idea of equality, it is assumed that businessmen reap their own reward. They are permitted to become rich through the indulgence of their less-acquisitive contemporaries. They cannot expect because they do not deserve praise as well as wealth.

Likewise, there is scant public sympathy for those who try to make it on their own and fail. They are not applauded for their courage or doggedness, rather they are criticised for being foolhardy and flawed by greed. They are accepted back into the fold of secure institutions in the public and private sectors like prodigal sons returned. The remnants of what they created are buried without ceremony. There are no flowers in the corporate graveyard.

The belief that there is something disreputable or ignoble about business has important consequences for an economy struggling to modernise itself. If the prejudice runs deep enough it will infect the whole of society with a profound reluctance to take risks. There will be an insufficiency of bold initiatives and entrepreneurial adventures, a paucity of new industries in the manufacturing and service sectors and a general lack of diversity, and hence of adaptability, in the economy.

The damaging effect of the anti-business attitude is most serious in the educational establishment. Young and impressionable minds, in the care of teachers all of whom have rejected, more or less deliberately, a career in business, are especially sensitive to the general prejudice. They are encouraged to prepare themselves for more reputable careers in trade unions, the law, medicine, government, social work, the arts and in teaching itself.

It is impossible to estimate how many young people who have the qualities needed for a successful business career are seduced away each year from such a life by the attractions of the more 'respectable' occupations. But if the number is only one, there is a price to be paid in terms of society's power to create wealth. The price rises sharply during periods of rapid technological advance. A key requirement for an economy at such a time is that the intake of talented youngsters into wealth-creating areas should be maximised.

The anti-business attitude in Britain is, in my view, the most serious of the obstructions barring our way to a modern and suitably disintegrated economy. It is very hard indeed to change a deep-rooted attitude like this, but if the attempt is to be made it is necessary first to reach some understanding of the origins of the attitude that is to be changed. It seems to me that the origins of the British anti-business attitude are partly economic and partly political.

John Maynard Keynes must bear the heaviest responsibility for the economic aspect, for he was the first to suggest that economic health could be achieved by enlightened government. Ever since the publication in 1936 of Keynes's *The General Theory of Employment, Interest and Money*, the underlying assumption has been that if we could only understand fully how our economy works and if we could acquire control over the variables that seem important, we could construct 'ideal' economic policies – policies which would permit our economy to realise its full productive potential.

That this goal has so far eluded us, the argument continues, merely shows that we have not been diligent enough in our search for it. This assumption, that the control by government of such things as 'aggregate effective demand' and 'money supply', is the secret of economic health, has relegated the entrepreneur to the status of a pawn in the economic chess game, moving according to the direction of the major pieces like the Treasury, the Bank of England and the money ministers of the Cabinet.

But after forty years of 'macroeconomic' management, what is there to show for it? How confident can we be that the indifferent record to date will improve and usher in a golden age of prosperous stability? Are we even still so sure that the macroeconomic problem – which is to achieve high growth accompanied by stable prices – is capable of solution? There are problems which are not.

Nuclear physics learned that lesson more than half a century ago when Werner Heisenberg enunciated his 'Uncertainty Principle' which states that it is not possible to determine simultaneously both the position and the momentum of a body. At any one time you can state one or the other, but not both. Many of Heisenberg's contemporaries, including Albert Einstein, found this conclusion unacceptable. It seemed to them untidy and inelegant. Einstein himself spent much of the latter part of his life trying to disprove it. But the uncertainty principle worked; it had explanatory power in the microcosmic world and it remains an integral part of the science of nuclear physics.

A few years later mathematics, which after Heisenberg had become the last refuge for those seeking certainty, was subjected to a similar shock. The foundations of mathematical certainty had begun to be undermined a century earlier when Lobachevski and Bolyai shattered the old certainty of Euclidian geometry by showing that there were also an infinite number of non-Euclidian geometries. Mathematicians swallowed that with a little difficulty and immediately threw themselves into the task of accommodating these unorthodox systems in a new synthesis.

One of the most heroic of these attempts was that of the

German mathematician Gotlob Frege. The second and final volume of his treatise on mathematics and symbolic logic was completed and on the point of publication when on June 16, 1902 a young English aristocrat, Bertrand Russell, wrote to him, pointing out that the argument in the first volume contained a paradox. Russell attempted to make good his destruction of Frege's work by embarking on a new attempt at synthesis in partnership with Alfred North Whitehead. The final part of their *Principia Mathematica* was published in 1913, and for twenty years afterwards it seemed that mathematical certainty had been successfully retrieved.

But then in 1933 the Austrian mathematician Kurt Gödel proved that the *Principia* was flawed too. He showed that it was consistent but incomplete and he went on to enunciate his 'Incompleteness Theorem' which states that every system, however complex, will always contain unresolvable paradoxes of the kind Russell used to puncture Frege's work. The incompleteness theorem does not mean that no problem is soluble; indeed, there are a vast, perhaps infinite, number of very complex problems to which solutions are available. What Gödel did was to show that there are two classes of problem, one of which contains difficulties which can be resolved given adequate information, and one of which contains difficulties to which there are no solutions no matter how much information is available.

There is a problem like this in the Keynesian system. 'Ideal' policies in the Keynesian sense are directed at controlling 'aggregate effective demand'. The idea is that if an economy is in recession it can be levered out of it by 'printing' more money – by creating wealth, with the stroke of a pen, where none before existed.

But Keynesian policies rely for their effectiveness on what is known as the 'money illusion'. Once the belief that price levels are fixed is dispelled, pumping more money into an economy begins to affect the price level as well as the level of economic activity. Eventually, when there is no illusion left, all the extra money feeds through into prices and economic activity remains unaffected.

Monetarism is also tainted by Gödel-type problems. How can you persuade people that your aim is to get the economy moving forward when you keep putting it into reverse? How can you control money supply by setting targets for the growth of monetary aggregates when the nature of those aggregates changes as soon as you start trying to control them?

The evidence is growing that macroeconomics is grappling with problems of the Gödel kind – problems that are fundamentally insoluble. That does not mean that there is no role for macroeconomics; it means merely that the ambitions of macroeconomists should be more modest. But even if this is accepted – even if economists yield their position as the primary wealth-creating agents to the entrepreneurs as I believe they should – the political aspects of the anti-business attitude in Britain will remain.

And these political origins of the attitude are much more intractable because they are based not on theories that are falsifiable but on beliefs which are not. The contemporary debate about nationalisation illustrates how beliefs of this kind operate.

The doctrine that state-ownership of an economy's 'commanding heights', and even of its foothills, is desirable in principle cannot be dismissed as mere political dogma. If that was all there was to it, then the abundantly apparent costs of collectivism, in terms of relative economic performance, would long ago have disabused the electorates of the west of the desirability of wholesale nationalisation. The fact that large and vocal sections of the British electorate still believe in a dominant public sector indicates a widespread conviction that state-ownership is not merely good in itself but that it also brings with it tangible benefits.

It seems to me though that these perceived benefits are negative – that what inclines so many towards the idea of an extension of the public sector is to do not so much with its positive benefits as with a deep and abiding distaste for and distrust of the private sector. And there is no denying that recent history provides cause for such anti-business attitudes, particularly in the small but powerful community of the multinational corporations.

The credulity of third-world populations has been cynically and cruelly exploited by Western producers of baby milk; the persistent cash-cropping by multinationals of their African estates has had tragic consequences for local inhabitants; one

US multinational has been clearly implicated in attempts to 'destabilise' an unsympathetic regime in a foreign country; the oil industry has obstinately refused to remove toxic pollutants from petrol; drug companies have been guilty of appalling negligence in their testing procedures with sometimes tragic results for their customers; banks and other large companies have been blithely dismissive of national prejudices against racist regimes.

Every advocate of more nationalisation will cite indignantly their own favourite examples of corporate irresponsibility. They will have endless tales of corruption, foul play, fraud, criminal negligence, theft – a whole litany of wickedness. After a while the overwhelming weight of anecdotal evidence, much of which is in my view valid and admissible, will have its inevitable consequence. The evidence will reach critical mass and the indictments of individual businesses will take a quantum jump and become an indictment of business in general.

I believe this has happened in Britain. For many people, too many, business has shown itself over the past few decades to be fundamentally untrustworthy and thus in need of strict control by the state.

And what better way is there to control than to possess?

I oppose nationalisation because I do not believe it is an effective answer to corporate crime and I reject the generalised anti-business attitude because I believe that the natural amorality of companies, which is a consequence of a company's responsibility to its shareholders, only becomes a problem when a company becomes very large. Before that stage is reached, at which point special arrangements to control overmighty companies should be made, there is a broad spectrum of tiny, small, medium and fairly large companies which comprise the vast bulk of the corporate population. It is here, in the heart of the economy, where the anti-business attitude, in its general form, causes so much damage.

But the strand of validity in the anti-business attitude – the extent to which it reflects accurately the people's sense of social justice and fair-play – makes it very hard to change or modify. It is not enough merely to stress the importance of efficiency, international competitiveness and a high rate of economic growth. These are public 'goods' which are recognised as such by all rational people. It must be demonstrated that the sacrifices in terms of prosperity that we are called on to make in the name of social justice are excessive; that in fact the interests of social justice would be *better* served by a more positive attitude to business.

But what is social justice? Is it the utilitarian dictum of Jeremy Bentham, that 'the greatest happiness of the greatest number is the foundation of morals and legislation', or should we incline more to so-called 'Pareto optimality' which enjoins us to constrain the Benthamite formula by requiring that the greatest happiness of the greatest number should not be achieved at the expense of the unhappiness of the few?

And if we do adopt the Pareto principle, how do we resolve the problems associated with a dynamic economy and the passage of time? Is half a loaf today worth more or less than one loaf tomorrow? Is the poverty of this generation a fair price to pay for the comfort of the next? Is it fair on future generations if those alive today squander 'God given' endowments such as North Sea oil in a ravenous rush for high but unsuitable living standards? Should the principle of 'finders keepers' apply, or do parts of such endowments properly belong to our children and our children's children? Do we have the right to burden our descendants with what may turn out to be an insoluble technical problem – the safe, long-term storage of radioactive waste?

I mention these questions not to offer answers to them but to demonstrate how difficult it is to arrive at a simple, generally acceptable principle of social justice. We are not dealing with self-evident truths. Opinion is divided not because some have better information than others but because there genuinely are a number of rational ways of looking at the same collection of facts.

The problem of social justice is of the Godel type. It is insoluble. There is no unique arrangement that all people at all times would regard as being fair. The fact of this insolubility, though seldom acknowledged as such, has caused the economic debate to become doctrinal. We espouse or reject the idea of more state-ownership or steeply progressive direct taxation according to our political prejudices. Economics has become the servant of politics. Since there is no unique solution we feel forced to adopt a point of view.

The trouble is that points of view these days come, like many other things, in packages; if you are in favour of an extension of nationalisation you are automatically assumed to be in favour also of more progressive rates of taxation, higher public spending, withdrawal from the Common Market, the abolition of private education, unilateral nuclear disarmament, import controls and Keynesian economic policies. If you are in favour of de-nationalisation you are, by the 'package' definition, a supporter of the free market, a multilateralist if not an out-and-out militarist, an ally of 'the bosses', a defender of privilege in all its forms and an advocate of monetarist economic policies.

I am in favour of the free market because I believe that in a changing, Gödel-world it is the best means available for the efficient allocation of resources. I support the principle of industrial common-ownership because I believe the co-operative attitude to work generated by a common-ownership structure is the one most closely attuned to the natural inclinations of the human spirit. I am a unilateralist because I feel in my bones that the fewer nuclear weapons there are in the world, the better.

According to the conventional cross-classification of ideas, which is organised along party political lines, my beliefs and preferences are hopelessly muddled; I cannot possibly believe in the free market *and* in common-ownership because the former is of the right wing of politics and the latter is of the left. Is there not a way out of this package trap, this insistent branding of people with some multi-faceted political label or other?

Even if there is no unique solution to the problem of social justice, there is certainly an optimal solution – one that takes into account as many of the people's conflicting wants and beliefs as possible. The culling of policies from packaged beliefs inhibits the achievement of this optimum by preventing each issue from being weighed individually.

And to the extent that doctrinaire policies result in a sub-optimal solution, there is a loss of welfare; and as soon as there is a loss of welfare one has a moral problem on one's hands – why has this welfare been squandered? Could not part of it at least have been deployed in improving the lot of the poor?

If there was only some way of breaking the grip of doctrine on popular economic attitudes, then perhaps some young people might not feel such antipathy towards business and might even be attracted to the idea of becoming an entrepreneur. If the anti-business attitude is to be refuted effectively, two things must be demonstrated: first, that the attitude does result in a significant loss of welfare and second that the loss can be recouped, i.e. that the anti-business attitude can be rejected, without comprising unduly all that is valid and admirable in the philosophy which has given rise to it.

I do not propose to attempt to demonstrate here that there is a loss of welfare associated with the anti-business attitude – that I believe there to be such a loss and that I believe it to be substantial is implicit in more or less everything I have said so far. But can it be re-couped? Is there some theory of justice which would permit socially-conscious people to abandon their anti-business attitudes without feeling they were betraying the ideals of their youth?

I believe that the American philosopher John Rawls provided just such a way of looking at the world with the publication in 1971 of his book *A Theory of Justice*. Rawls proposes, in effect, that the question 'What is just?' should be replaced by the question 'How can we so organise our society that no decisions are taken which appear to some people to be manifestly unjust?'*

In his search for an answer to the new question Rawls adopts what is known as a 'contractarian' approach (after Rousseau's *Social Contract*). It goes something like this: 'If a collection of people were brought together in a dark room, knowing nothing about the world outside, nothing about each other and nothing about themselves – their attitudes, their physical attributes and their hereditary endowment – are there any principles which they would all agree to as being fair and as constituting a workable basis for regulating all further agreements after they leave the dark room and begin to live together in a society?'

Rawls concludes that there are two such principles. One of

* The form of this substitution is based on a similar confrontation of old and new questions posed by Sir Karl Popper in Volume 1 of *The Open Society and its Enemies*. Popper suggested there that the question 'Who should rule?' must be replaced by the question 'How can we so organise political institutions that bad or incompetent rulers can be prevented from doing too much damage?'

his many formulations of them is: 'All social primary goods – liberty and opportunity, income and wealth, and the basis of self-respect – are to be distributed equally unless an unequal distribution of any or all of these goods is to the advantage of the least favoured.' This focusses attention firmly on the poor. In Rawls's view it is the predicament of the poor which makes the idea of equality meaningful and he argues that the interests of the poor should be paramount when it comes to assessing what degree of inequality is tolerable.

When the National Enterprise Board announced plans to invest substantial sums of public money in the Inmos silicon chip company, left-wing politicians expressed deep disapproval on the grounds that the way the company was structured made it inevitable, in the event of it prospering, that a small group of people would become very wealthy. They felt that this added inequality was, by itself, sufficient reason to object to the plan.

Rawls would disagree. He would argue that if a successful Inmos generated sufficient tax and investment income to offset the original investment, and that if it would be shown that no other use of the public funds concerned would have been likely to generate such a substantial increase in revenue, then it would be in the interests of the poor to approve the plan irrespective of whether or not a small number of entrepreneurs became as rich as Croesus in the process. In the Rawlsian scheme this would have been an admissible breach of the equality principle because the inequality it created would have been 'to the advantage of the least favoured'.

A more general illustration of the point is provided when we apply the Rawlsian principles to the idea of progressive income tax. The purpose of a progressive income tax system is to redistribute income from the rich to the poor; its disadvantage is that high rates of income tax act as a disincentive to wealth-creating activity. Taking it for granted that more equality, and thus some degree of progression in income tax are desirable, where do we fix the trade-off between the 'good' of a fairer distribution and the 'bad' of a lower rate of wealth creation?

According to Rawls the trade-off should be fixed by the poor, or by reference to the interests of the poor. He suggests, if you please, that politicians should go out and ask the poor how rich the rich should be allowed to be. Armed with his principles,

Rawls sets about re-organising society. The first task is to establish what he calls 'background fairness'. This will be obtained by a just constitution securing the liberties of equal citizenship, liberty of conscience, freedom of thought and the laying down of just procedures for choosing governments and enacting legislation. Equality of opportunity is achieved by such things as free or subsidised education, free choice of occupation (which might require laws against racist or sexist discrimination in the labour market) and tough anti-monopoly measures. Government guarantees of a minimum standard of living are also important for background fairness and can be achieved by such things as family allowances, payments during periods of sickness or unemployment or by something like a negative income tax.

Rawls sees a number of functionally distinct branches of government at work during the task of establishing background fairness.

First, there is the *allocation branch* which is responsible for making the price system 'workably competitive' and for preventing the emergence of 'unreasonable market power'. Then there is the *stabilisation branch* which is charged with the task of achieving reasonably full employment in a situation where there is free choice of occupation. These two branches together are responsible for maintaining what Rawls calls 'the efficiency of the market economy'.

The maintenance of a social minimum standard of living is the responsibility of the *transfer branch*. This is needed because, as Rawls points out, 'a competitive price system gives no consideration to needs and therefore it cannot be the sole device of distribution.'

Fourthly, there is the *distribution branch*. Whereas the transfer branch is concerned to ensure that everyone enjoys a reasonable standard of living, the distribution branch is responsible for achieving fair shares of what is left once the minimum standard has generally been reached. The distribution branch has two jobs. First it imposes inheritance and gift taxes not to raise revenue but to correct any imbalances 'detrimental to the fair value of political liberty and fair equality of opportunity'. Second, it is responsible for devising a tax system to raise the revenue needed to provide public goods and to finance the payments made by the transfer branch. It will need to ensure that the burden of taxation is shared fairly.

(Rawls suggests, in passing, that 'a proportional expenditure tax may be part of the best tax scheme . . . since it imposes a levy according to how much a person takes out of the common store of goods and not according to how much he contributes.')

This division of function between various 'branches' of government is an interesting idea. It suggests, for example, that there may be nothing inconsistent about a concern for social justice on the one hand and a belief that the top rates of a progressive tax system are too high on the other. It implies that policy-makers should be required, by the principles of justice, to keep in mind at all times the distinction between the allocative and distributive functions. There will inevitably be overlaps; policies designed to improve the allocation of resources and the efficient working of markets will have implications for the distribution branch of government, and vice versa. But if the Rawlsian principles are accepted, there would be no need for allocative and distributive policies to be as hopelessly confused as they are at present.

And neither would there be any justification for writers like J. K. Galbraith to ridicule the ideas of 'supply-side' economists (of which, I suppose, I am one) as boiling down to the proposition that people doing interesting jobs which they enjoy should be paid more than those doing boring jobs which they hate. Supply-side economists are concerned with the allocation branch of government. Their job is to identify areas where there are market inefficiencies and to suggest ways of correcting them. They are not, as they are sometimes depicted, the apologists of the rich and the enemies of equality; at least not all of them are and none of them are by definition. A belief that the size of the cake should be maximised is not at all inconsistent with a belief that the cake should be shared out fairly. The fact that supply-side economics has nothing to say about fair shares does not mean that all supply-side economists care nothing for equality and social justice.

A modern, prosperous and civilised society needs political philosophers *and* entrepreneurs – it needs a political philosophy that makes due acknowledgment of the importance of wealth- and employment-creating activity. A society which regards entrepreneurs as disreputable aberrations from the norm, as money-grubbing and predatory, is unlikely to perform very well economically during the era of rapid technological advance.

Select Bibliography

Blackaby, Frank (ed.), *De-Industrialisation*, Heinemann/NIESR, 1978.

Bullock, Matthew, *Academic Enterprise, Industrial Innovation and the Development* of *High Technology Financing in the United States*, Brand Brothers & Co., 1983.

Evans, Christopher, *The Mighty Micro*, Gollancz, 1979.

Forrester, Tom (ed.), *The Microelectronics Revolution*, Basil Blackwell, 1980.

Gould, Stephen Jay, *Ever since Darwin: Reflections in Natural History*, Deutsch, 1978.

Hofstadter, Douglas, *Godel, Escher and Bach. An Eternal Golden Braid*, Harvester, 1979.

Ouchi, William, *Theory Z. How American Business can meet the Japanese Challenge*, Addison-Wesley. 1981.

Pavitt, Keith (ed.), *Technical Innovation and British Economic Performance*, Macmillan, 1980.

Rawls, John, *A Theory of Justice*, Oxford University Press, 1973.

Schumacher, E. F., *Small is Beautiful*, Blond & Briggs, 1973.

Toffler, Alvin, *The Third Wave*, Collins, 1980.

Index

For Product Safety Concerns and Information please contact our EU
representative GPSR@taylorandfrancis.com
Taylor & Francis Verlag GmbH, Kaufingerstraße 24, 80331 München, Germany

www.ingramcontent.com/pod-product-compliance
Ingram Content Group UK Ltd.
Pitfield, Milton Keynes, MK11 3LW, UK
UKHW020159200926
475702UK00004B/537

* 9 7 8 1 0 4 1 3 5 4 0 8 6 *